PRENTICE HALL
EXPL⦿RING
Physical Science

LABORATORY MANUAL

Prentice Hall
Englewood Cliffs, New Jersey
Needham, Massachusetts

Laboratory Manual

PRENTICE HALL
Exploring Physical Science

ISBN 0-13-807133-0

3 4 5 6 7 8 9 10   98 97 96 95

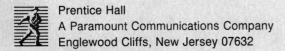
Prentice Hall
A Paramount Communications Company
Englewood Cliffs, New Jersey 07632

Contents

Safety Symbols

All the investigations in this *Laboratory Manual* have been designed with safety in mind. If you follow the instructions, you should have a safe and interesting year in the laboratory. Before beginning any investigation, make sure you read the safety rules that follow.

The eight safety symbols below appear next to certain steps in some of the investigations in this *Laboratory Manual*. The symbols alert you to the need for special safety precautions. The description of each symbol below tells you which precautions to take whenever you see the symbol in an investigation.

Glassware Safety

1. Whenever you see this symbol, you will know that you are working with glassware that can easily be broken. Take particular care to handle such glassware safely. And never use broken or chipped glassware.
2. Never heat glassware that is not thoroughly dry. Never pick up any glassware unless you are sure it is not hot. If it is hot, use heat-resistant gloves.
3. Always clean glassware thoroughly before putting it away.

Fire Safety

1. Whenever you see this symbol, you will know that you are working with fire. Never use any source of fire without wearing safety goggles.
2. Never heat anything—particularly chemicals—unless instructed to do so.
3. Never heat anything in a closed container.
4. Never reach across a flame.
5. Always use a clamp, tongs, or heat-resistant gloves to handle hot objects.
6. Always maintain a clean work area, particularly when using a flame.

Heat Safety

Whenever you see this symbol, you will know that you should put on heat-resistant gloves to avoid burning your hands.

Chemical Safety

1. Whenever you see this symbol, you will know that you are working with chemicals that could be hazardous.
2. Never smell any chemical directly from its container. Always use your hand to waft some of the odors from the top of the container toward your nose—and only when instructed to do so.
3. Never mix chemicals unless instructed to do so.
4. Never touch or taste any chemical unless instructed to do so.
5. Keep all lids closed when chemicals are not in use. Dispose of all chemicals as instructed by your teacher.
6. Immediately rinse with water any chemicals, particularly acids, that get on your skin and clothes. Then notify your teacher.

Eye and Face Safety

1. Whenever you see this symbol, you will know that you are performing an experiment in which you must take precautions to protect your eyes and face by wearing safety goggles.
2. When you are heating a test tube or bottle, always point it away from you and others. Chemicals can splash or boil out of a heated test tube.

Sharp Instrument Safety

1. Whenever you see this symbol, you will know that you are working with a sharp instrument.
2. Always use single-edged razors; double-edged razors are too dangerous.
3. Handle any sharp instrument with extreme care. Never cut any material toward you; always cut away from you.
4. Immediately notify your teacher if your skin is cut.

Electrical Safety

1. Whenever you see this symbol, you will know that you are using electricity in the laboratory.
2. Never use long extension cords to plug in any electrical device. Do not plug too many appliances into one socket or you may overload the socket and cause a fire.
3. Never touch an electrical appliance or outlet with wet hands.

Animal Safety

1. Whenever you see this symbol, you will know that you are working with live animals.
2. Do not cause pain, discomfort, or injury to an animal.
3. Follow your teacher's directions when handling animals. Wash your hands thoroughly after handling animals or their cages.

Science Safety Rules

One of the first things a scientist learns is that working in the laboratory can be an exciting experience. But the laboratory can also be quite dangerous if proper safety rules are not followed at all times. To prepare yourself for a safe year in the laboratory, read over the following safety rules. Then read them a second time. Make sure you understand each rule. If you do not, ask your teacher to explain any rules you are unsure of.

Dress Code

1. Many materials in the laboratory can cause eye injury. To protect yourself from possible injury, wear safety goggles whenever you are working with chemicals, burners, or any substance that might get into your eyes. Never wear contact lenses in the laboratory.
2. Wear a laboratory apron or coat whenever you are working with chemicals or heated substances.
3. Tie back long hair to keep it away from any chemicals, burners, and candles, or other laboratory equipment.
4. Remove or tie back any article of clothing or jewelry that can hang down and touch chemicals and flames.

General Safety Rules

5. Read all directions for an experiment several times. Follow the directions exactly as they are written. If you are in doubt about any part of the experiment, ask your teacher for assistance.
6. Never perform activities that are not authorized by your teacher. Obtain permission before "experimenting" on your own.
7. Never handle any equipment unless you have specific permission.
8. Take extreme care not to spill any material in the laboratory. If a spill occurs, immediately ask your teacher about the proper cleanup procedure. Never simply pour chemicals or other substances into the sink or trash container.
9. Never eat in the laboratory.
10. Wash your hands before and after each experiment.

First Aid

11. Immediately report all accidents, no matter how minor, to your teacher.
12. Learn what to do in case of specific accidents, such as getting acid in your eyes or on your skin. (Rinse acids from your body with lots of water.)
13. Become aware of the location of the first-aid kit. But your teacher should administer any required first aid due to injury. Or your teacher may send you to the school nurse or call a physician.
14. Know where and how to report an accident or fire. Find out the location of the fire extinguisher, phone, and fire alarm. Keep a list of important phone numbers—such as the fire department and the school nurse —near the phone. Immediately report any fires to your teacher.

Heating and Fire Safety

15. Again, never use a heat source, such as a candle or a burner, without wearing safety goggles.
16. Never heat a chemical you are not instructed to heat. A chemical that is harmless when cool may be dangerous when heated.
17. Maintain a clean work area and keep all materials away from flames.
18. Never reach across a flame.
19. Make sure you know how to light a Bunsen burner. (Your teacher will demonstrate the proper procedure for lighting a burner.) If the flame leaps out of a burner toward you, immediately turn off the gas. Do not touch the burner. It may be hot. And never leave a lighted burner unattended!
20. When heating a test tube or bottle, always point it away from you and others. Chemicals can splash or boil out of a heated test tube.

21. Never heat a liquid in a closed container. The expanding gases produced may blow the container apart, injuring you or others.
22. Before picking up a container that has been heated, first hold the back of your hand near it. If you can feel the heat on the back of your hand, the container may be too hot to handle. Use a clamp or tongs when handling hot containers.

Using Chemicals Safely

23. Never mix chemicals for the "fun of it." You might produce a dangerous, possibly explosive substance.
24. Never touch, taste, or smell a chemical unless you are instructed by your teacher to do so. Many chemicals are poisonous. If you are instructed to note the fumes in an experiment, gently wave your hand over the opening of a container and direct the fumes toward your nose. Do not inhale the fumes directly from the container.
25. Use only those chemicals needed in the activity. Keep all lids closed when a chemical is not being used. Notify your teacher whenever chemicals are spilled.
26. Dispose of all chemicals as instructed by your teacher. To avoid contamination, never return chemicals to their original containers.
27. Be extra careful when working with acids or bases. Pour such chemicals over the sink, not over your workbench.
28. When diluting an acid, pour the acid into water. Never pour water into the acid.
29. Immediately rinse with water any acids that get on your skin or clothing. Then notify your teacher of any acid spill.

Using Glassware Safely

30. Never force glass tubing into a rubber stopper. A turning motion and lubricant will be helpful when inserting glass tubing into rubber stoppers or rubber tubing. Your teacher will demonstrate the proper way to insert glass tubing.
31. Never heat glassware that is not thoroughly dry. Use a wire screen to protect glassware from any flame.
32. Keep in mind that hot glassware will not appear hot. Never pick up glassware without first checking to see if it is hot. See #22.
33. If you are instructed to cut glass tubing, fire-polish the ends immediately to remove sharp edges.
34. Never use broken or chipped glassware. If glassware breaks, notify your teacher and dispose of the glassware in the proper trash container.
35. Never eat or drink from laboratory glassware.
36. Thoroughly clean glassware before putting it away.

Using Sharp Instruments

37. Handle scalpels or razor blades with extreme care. Never cut material toward you; cut away from you.
38. Immediately notify your teacher if you cut your skin when working in the laboratory.

Animal Safety

39. No experiments that cause pain, discomfort, or harm to mammals, birds, reptiles, fish, and amphibians should be done in the classroom or at home.
40. Animals should be handled only if necessary. If an animal is excited or frightened, pregnant, feeding, or with its young, special handling is required.
41. Your teacher will instruct you as to how to handle each animal species that may be brought into the classroom.
42. Clean your hands thoroughly after handling animals or the cage containing animals.

End-of-Experiment Rules

43. After an experiment has been completed, clean up your work area and return all equipment to its proper place.
44. Wash your hands after every experiment.
45. Turn off all candles and burners before leaving the laboratory. Check that the gas line leading to the burner is off as well.

Laboratory Skills Checkup 1 _____

Following Directions

1. Read all of the following directions before you do anything.

2. Print your name, last name first then your first name and middle initial (if you have one), at the top of this page.

3. Draw a line through the word "all" in direction 1.

4. Underline the word "directions" in direction 1.

5. In direction 2, circle the words "your first name."

6. In direction 3, place an "X" in front of the word "through."

7. Cross out the numbers of the even-numbered directions above.

8. In direction 7, cross out the word "above" and write the word "below" above it.

9. Write "Following directions is easy" under your name at the top of this page.

10. In direction 9, add the following sentence after the word "page." "That's what you think!"

11. Draw a square in the upper right-hand corner of this page.

12. Draw a triangle in the lower left-hand corner of this page.

13. Place a circle in the center of the square.

14. Place an "X" in the center of the triangle.

15. Now that you have read all the directions as instructed in direction 1, follow directions 2 and 16 only.

16. Please do not give away what this test is about by saying anything or doing anything to alert your classmates. If you have reached this direction, make believe you are still writing. See how many of your classmates really know how to follow directions.

Laboratory Skills Checkup 2 _____

Defining Elements of a
Scientific Method

Laboratory activities and experiments involve the use of the scientific method. Listed in the left column are the names of parts of this method. The right column contains definitions. Next to each word in the left column, place the letter of the definition that best matches.

Conclusion   A. What the person performing the activity sees, hears, smells, or tastes

Control   B. Gathering information about the subject of the activity

Data   C. Proposed explanation for a problem or observation

Hypothesis   D. Factor being tested

Objective   E. Measurements

Observation   F. Result of a laboratory activity

Research   G. Problem that the laboratory activity is designed to solve

Variable   H. Experiment with the variable left out

Laboratory Skills Checkup 3 _____

Analyzing Elements of the Scientific Method

Read the following statements and then answer the questions.

1. You have just bought an old-fashioned clock that runs by weights on chains and a pendulum.

2. To get the clock to run, you pull the weights up and start the pendulum swinging. Your watch says 4:00 so you set the clock to this time.

3. Several hours later, you return with a friend to look at your clock. According to your watch it is 8:05, but the clock reads 8:15.

4. After determining that there is nothing wrong with your watch, your friend asks, "What do you think caused the clock to gain time?"

5. You watch the clock for a few minutes and then propose, "I think that if the pendulum swings too quickly, it makes the clock run fast."

6. You continue, "I also think that if the length of the pendulum were increased, the pendulum would swing more slowly and the clock would run on time."

7. "Furthermore," you say, "to test my explanation, I will suspend strings of three different lengths and tie a washer to the end of each. Then, I will swing each length of string from a 45° angle and time how quickly each swings."

Questions

A. In which statement is a **prediction** made? _____

B. Which statement states a **problem**? _____

C. In which statement is an **experiment** described? _____

D. Which statement contains a **hypothesis**? _____

E. Which statements contain **data**? _____

F. Which statement describes **observations**? _____

Laboratory Skills Checkup 4 _____

Performing an Experiment

Read the following statements and then answer the questions.

1. A scientist notices that her pendulum-powered clock is running fast. She wants to find out why.

2. Since the scientist has misplaced the clock's instructions, she goes to the library and reads some books about clocks.

3. The scientist learns that the swinging pendulum controls how quickly the clock hands move. The faster the pendulum swings, the faster the hands go.

4. In light of this information, the scientist guesses that if the pendulum were longer, it would not swing quite as fast.

5. The scientist goes to her laboratory to test her idea. She does the following:

   a. Suspends a string 1 meter long from the ring of a ring stand.
   b. Ties a washer to the end of the string.
   c. Raises the washer to a 45° angle and lets it go.
   d. Records in her notebook the time it takes the washer to make each of the first five swings.
   e. Repeats the procedure using a string 0.50 meter long and 0.25 meter long.

6. The scientist writes in her notebook, "The meter-long pendulum swings two times slower than the 0.25-meter-long pendulum and about one and a half times slower than the 0.50-meter-long pendulum."

7. The scientist finishes her report stating, "It appears that a longer pendulum swings more slowly. Therefore, if I increase the length of the pendulum on my clock, the pendulum will swing more slowly and the clock will not run as fast."

Questions

A. Which statement contains a **conclusion**? _____

B. Which statements refer to **research**? _____

C. Which statement contains a **hypothesis**? _____

D. Which statements describe **observations** being made? _____

E. Which statement describes an **experiment**? _____

F. Which statement **supports** the **hypothesis**? _____

G. In which statement is the **problem** defined? _____

H. Which statements contain **data**? _____

I. What is the **variable** in the experiment? _____

J. What is the **control** in the experiment? _____

K. Which statement contains a **generalization**? _____

Laboratory Skills Checkup 5 _____

Identifying Errors

Read the following paragraph and then answer the questions.

Sandy arrived at school and went directly to his physical science class. His teacher gave him a thermometer, a beaker of ice, and a small jar of potassium nitrate, a type of salt. The teacher asked Sandy to determine the amount of salt that would dissolve in 100 mL of water at 5°C. Sandy filled a beaker with 100 mL of water and placed it in the beaker of ice. He cooled the water to 5°C and left the beaker of water in the ice. Sandy next poured some salt onto the pan of the laboratory balance. He measured out 1.5 grams and committed the number to memory. After brushing the salt into his hand, Sandy slowly added it to the water, stirring occasionally with the thermometer. When no more salt would dissolve, he poured the remaining salt back onto the balance pan. By looking at the amount of salt in the pan, Sandy estimated that about 1 gram was left.

Questions

1. Why will Sandy have trouble calculating the amount of potassium nitrate dissolved in the water?

   _____

   _____

2. What was wrong with pouring the salt onto the balance pan and his hand? _____

   _____

   _____

3. What was wrong with Sandy's stirring method? _____

   _____

4. What mistake did Sandy make when taking the water's temperature? _____

   _____

   _____

5. What was wrong with Sandy's final measurement of the amount of salt?

   _____

   _____

   _____

Laboratory Skills Checkup 6

Making Measurements

Look at the drawings and write the letter of the drawing next to the description that it matches.

1. Measures time _____

2. Measures weight _____

3. Measures mass _____

4. Measures volume _____

5. Measures air pressure _____

6. Measures temperature _____

7. Measures length _____

8. Measures electric current _____

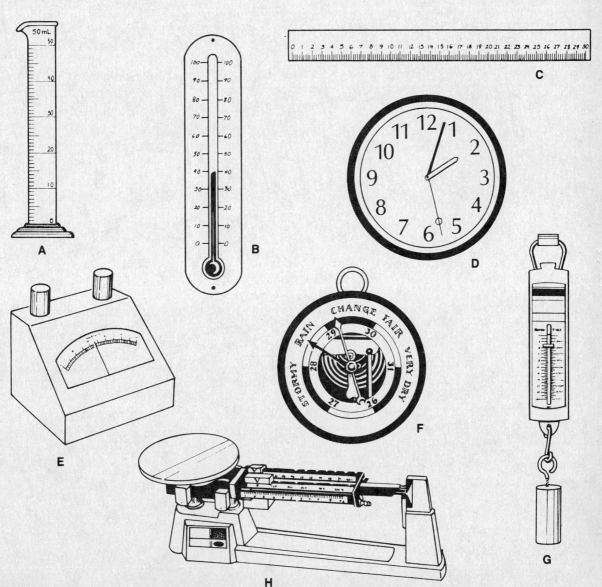

Laboratory Skills Checkup 7 _____

Safety First

Circle any drawing that shows an unsafe laboratory activity and explain why it is unsafe.

_____

_____

_____

_____

_____

_____

_____

_____

_____

_____

_____

_____

_____

_____

_____

_____

_____

_____

_____

_____

Laboratory Investigation

Chapter 1 Exploring Physical Science   **1**

Metric Measurement: Volume and Temperature

Background Information

The amount of space an object takes up is called its volume. The basic unit of volume is the liter (L). Smaller volumes are measured in milliliters (mL), or 1/1000 of a liter. In the laboratory, the graduated cylinder is used to measure the volume of liquids.

Temperature is measured with a thermometer. The unit of measurement for temperature is degrees Celsius (°C).

In this investigation you will learn how to accurately measure the volume and temperature of a liquid.

Problem

How can you accurately measure the volume and temperature of a liquid?

Materials *(per group)*

water
2 100-mL beakers
100-mL graduated cylinder
glass-marking pencil
2 Celsius thermometers
ice cubes

Procedure

Part A Measuring the Volume of a Liquid

🜂 1. Fill a beaker half full of water.

2. Pour the water in the beaker into the graduated cylinder.

3. Measure the amount of water in the graduated cylinder. To accurately measure the volume, your eye must be at the same level as the bottom of the meniscus. The meniscus is the curved surface of a column of liquid. See Figure 1.

4. Record the volume of water to the nearest mL in Data Table 1.

5. Repeat steps 1 through 4 with a beaker that is one fourth full of water.

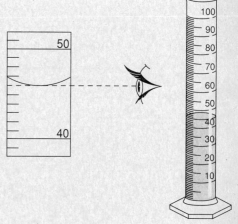

Figure 1

Part B Measuring the Temperature of a Liquid

🜂 1. With the glass-marking pencil, label the beakers A and B.

2. Fill both beakers with 50 mL of water. Record this volume in Data Table 2.

3. Place a thermometer in each beaker. Record the temperature of the water in each beaker in Data Table 3.

4. Carefully add three ice cubes to the water in beaker B.

5. After one minute, observe the temperature of the water in each beaker. Record the temperatures in Data Table 3.

6. After five minutes, observe the temperature of the water in each beaker. Record the temperatures in Data Table 3.

7. Find the volume of the water in beaker A. Record the volume in Data Table 2.

8. After the ice in beaker B has melted, find the volume of water. Record the volume in Data Table 2.

Observations

DATA TABLE 1

	Volume of Water (mL)
One half filled beaker	
One fourth filled beaker	

DATA TABLE 2

	Volume of Water (mL)	
	Beginning of Investigation	End of Investigation
Beaker A		
Beaker B		

DATA TABLE 3

	Temperature of Water (°C)		
	Beginning of Investigation	After 1 Minute	After 5 Minutes
Beaker A			
Beaker B			

Analysis and Conclusions

1. What is the largest volume of a liquid that your graduated cylinder is able to measure?

_____

2. What is the smallest volume of a liquid that your graduated cylinder is able to measure?

_____

3. Did the temperature of the water in beakers A and B change during the investigation?

Explain. _____

_____

_____

_____

_____

_____

4. Was there a difference in the volume of water in the beakers at the end of the

investigation? Explain. _____

_____

_____

_____

_____

Critical Thinking and Application

1. Of the following graduated cylinders, 100 mL, 25 mL, or 10 mL, which would you use to

accurately measure 8 mL of a liquid? Explain. _____

_____

_____

_____

_____

_____

2. Using a Celsius thermometer, how would you determine the temperature of your

classroom? _____

_____

_____

_____

_____

3. When ice was added to beaker B, the thermometer was not removed. Explain why.

_____

_____

_____

_____

_____

4. Suppose the water in beaker B had been stirred after the ice had been added. What would be the immediate effect of this on the temperature of the water? Would stirring have an effect on the final temperature of the water?

_____

_____

_____

_____

_____

_____

5. Why do you think the water in the graduated cylinder forms a meniscus?

_____

_____

_____

Going Further

Evaporation is sometimes described as a cooling process. This is because as a liquid evaporates it takes heat from the surroundings. Using water, two Celsius thermometers, a small piece of gauze, and some thread, design an investigation to test the statement. Indicate the control and the variable. Include problem, hypothesis, procedure, observations, and conclusions. With your teacher's permission, perform this investigation.

_____ *Laboratory Investigation* _____

Tools of the Scientist:
The Bunsen Burner and
a Filtering Apparatus

Part A   Using the Bunsen Burner
Background Information

Often a chemist needs to heat materials in a laboratory. One of the most efficient ways to do this is to use a Bunsen burner. Bunsen burners are made in a variety of designs. In every one, however, the burner functions by the combustion of a mixture of air and gas. In most burners, the amounts of air and gas can be controlled. In some situations, portable liquid-petroleum burners are used instead of Bunsen burners. Electric hot plates may be used as well.

In this investigation you will learn the parts of the Bunsen burner and their functions. You will also learn how to use the burner safely in the laboratory.

Problem

How can the Bunsen burner be safely used to heat materials in the laboratory?

Materials *(per group)*

Bunsen burner or portable   beaker tongs
  liquid-petroleum burner   iron ring
ring stand   safety goggles
2 250-mL beakers   100-mL graduated cylinder
wire gauze

Procedure

1. Examine your burner when it is not connected to the gas outlet. If your burner is the type that can easily be taken apart, unscrew the barrel from the base and locate the parts shown in Figure 1. If you are using a portable liquid-petroleum burner, see Figure 2. As you examine the parts, think about their functions.

   The **barrel** is the area where the air and gas mix.
   The **collar** can be turned to adjust the intake of air. If you turn the collar so that the holes are larger, more air will be drawn into the barrel.
   The **air intake openings** are the holes in the collar through which the air is drawn.
   The **base** supports the burner so that it does not tip over.
   The **gas intake tube** brings the supply of gas from the outlet to the burner.
   The **spud** is the small opening through which the gas flows. The small opening causes the gas to enter the barrel with great speed.

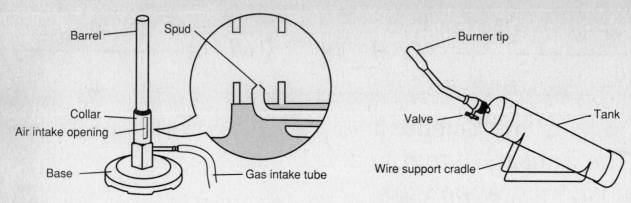

Barrel — Spud

Collar —
Air intake opening —

Base — Gas intake tube

Figure 1

Burner tip

Valve — Tank

Wire support cradle

Figure 2

2. Reassemble the Bunsen burner if necessary and connect the tube to the gas outlet. Put on safety goggles. Make sure that the burner is away from all flammable materials.

3. Adjust the collar so that the air intake openings are half open. Hold a lighted match about 2 cm above and just to the right of the barrel. Hold the match in this position while you open the gas valve slowly until it is fully open. The burner can be turned off by using the valve. Do not lean over the burner when lighting it.

4. Practice relighting the burner several times. Adjust the collar so that the flame is blue and a pale blue inner cone is visible.

5. Adjust the flow of gas until the flame is about 6 cm high. Some burners have a valve in the base to regulate the flow of gas, but the flow of gas can always be adjusted at the gas outlet valve. After adjusting the flow of gas, shut off the burner. Leave your safety goggles on as you proceed with step 6.

6. Arrange the apparatus as pictured in Figure 3.

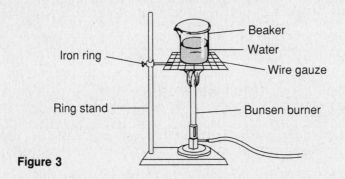

Iron ring — Beaker
— Water
— Wire gauze

Ring stand — Bunsen burner

Figure 3

7. Adjust the iron ring so that the bottom of the beaker is about 2 cm above the mouth of the barrel. Measure 100 mL of water in the graduated cylinder and pour it into the beaker.

8. Light the burner and heat the beaker. The bottom of the beaker should just be touching the top of the inner cone of the flame. Record the time it takes for the water to start boiling rapidly. Using the tongs, carefully remove the beaker.

9. Repeat the procedure with the other beaker at a height of about 6 cm above the mouth of the barrel. Record the time it takes for the water to start boiling rapidly at this height. Be sure that the starting temperature of the water is the same in each trial.

Observations

DATA TABLE

Height Above Burner (cm)	Time to Boil (min)
2	
6	

Analysis and Conclusions

1. What would happen if the air intake openings were made very small?

_____

_____

2. If the burner did not light even after the gas outlet valve was open, what might be

wrong? _____

3. Where is the hottest part of the flame? Where did the water boil the soonest?

_____

4. Why is it important to make sure that the volume of water and the starting temperature are the same in each trial?

_____

Part B Filtering
Background Information

Physical scientists are able to separate materials based on their differing properties. One of the techniques used quite often is filtering. In this activity you will learn how to separate a salt-and-sand mixture by adding water and filtering the mixture. The salt will be reclaimed.

Problem

How can a salt-and-sand mixture be separated?

Materials *(per group)*

Bunsen burner or	ring stand	wire gauze
portable liquid	safety goggles	evaporating dish
petroleum burner	glass stirring rod	tongs
filter paper	2 250-mL beakers	10 g salt-and-sand mixture
funnel	small iron ring	graduated cylinder

Procedure

🧪 1. Obtain a 10 g sample of salt-and-sand mixture from your teacher.

2. Add 50 mL of water to the salt-and-sand mixture in the beaker. Stir.

3. Prepare filter paper as shown in Figure 4. Fold a circle of filter paper across the middle. Fold the resulting half-circle to form a quarter-circle. Open the folded paper into a cone, leaving a triple layer on one side and a single layer on the other.

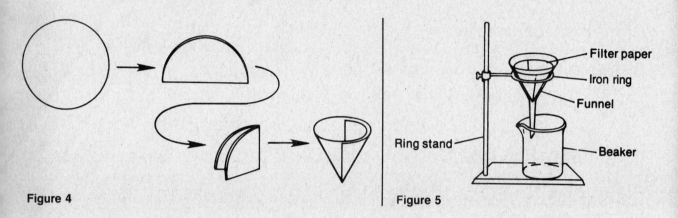

Figure 4 | Figure 5

4. Support a glass funnel as shown in Figure 5. Place the cone of the filter paper in the funnel and wet the paper so that it adheres smoothly to the walls of the funnel. Set a clean beaker beneath the funnel in such a way that the stem of the funnel touches the side of the beaker.

5. Pour the salt-sand-water mixture slowly into the funnel. Do not let the mixture overflow the filter paper.

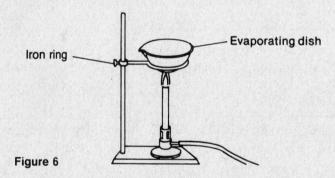

Figure 6

6. Carefully remove the filter paper from the funnel and dispose of it in the waste container provided by your teacher. Do not throw sand or filter paper in the sink.

🧪 7. Set up the evaporating dish and equipment as shown in Figure 6.

🔥 8. Pour some of the contents of the beaker into the evaporating dish. Put on your safety goggles. Heat the contents carefully. Do not let the solution boil over or spatter onto the table top. Turn off the burner when nearly all the liquid has evaporated.

Observations

When all the water has evaporated, what remains in the evaporating dish?

_____

_____

Analysis and Conclusions

1. What is the probable identity of the substance left in the evaporating dish?

_____

2. Could a mixture of sugar and salt be separated in the same way? Why or why not?

_____

_____

3. The material left in the filter paper is called the residue. If a mixture of chalk dust, salt, and water were poured through filter paper, what would the residue be?

_____

4. Could two liquids such as alcohol and water be separated this way? Why or why not?

_____

Critical Thinking and Application

1. A student heated a beaker containing a liquid over a yellow flame. After the beaker was removed, the student noticed a black deposit on the underside of the beaker.

   a. Where did the black deposit come from? _____

   _____

   _____

   b. What could the student do the next time to avoid having the black deposit?

   _____

   _____

2. State two reasons why a blue flame is preferred over a yellow flame in a Bunsen burner.

_____

_____

3. What safety precautions should be followed before lighting a burner?

_____

_____

_____

_____

_____

4. In what situation should the filter paper not be wet with water to make it adhere to the sides of the funnel? Why? _____

_____

_____

_____

Going Further

Test the ability of different kinds of laboratory burners to heat water to boiling. Determine if there is a difference in the efficiency with which different burners are able to heat objects.

Laboratory Investigation

Determining Density

Background Information

Which is heavier, a kilogram of lead or a kilogram of feathers? This is an old question with a simple answer. Since both objects have a mass of 1 kg, they are equally heavy. Each feather, however, has less mass than each piece of lead. So a greater number of feathers is needed to make a kilogram. And the more feathers there are, the more space they take up. The space an object occupies is its volume. So a kilogram of feathers has a greater volume than a kilogram of lead. The mass of a certain volume of feathers is different from the mass of the same volume of lead.

The mass of a specific volume of an object is called density. Density can be expressed mathematically as:

$$\text{Density} = \frac{\text{Mass}}{\text{Volume}}$$

Density is a property of all objects. In this investigation you will learn about this important characteristic.

Problem

How can the density of an object be determined?

Materials _(per group)_

triple-beam balance
metric ruler
100-mL graduated cylinder
2 rectangular solids of the same
   material but of different
   dimensions, such as a bar and
   a cube of iron, copper, or
   aluminum
1 large piece of modeling clay

Procedure
Part A   Density of Rectangular Solids

1. Using the balance, determine the mass of each solid. Follow the directions given by your teacher for the proper use of the balance. Read the mass of each solid to the nearest 0.1 g. Record your data in the appropriate column of Data Table 1.

2. Determine the volume of each solid using the metric ruler to measure length, width, and height. Read these values to the nearest 0.1 cm. Now use the formula for volume $V = L \times W \times H$, where L = length, W = width, and H = height, to calculate the volume of each solid. Add these data to Data Table 1.

3. Calculate the density of each sample, using the formula Density = Mass/Volume (D = M/V), and record your results in Data Table 1.

Part B Density of Irregular Solids

1. Separate the large piece of modeling clay into five pieces of different sizes. Make sure that the mass of the smallest sample is no less than 5 g.

2. Using the balance, determine the mass of each sample to the nearest 0.1 g. Record your data in the appropriate column of Data Table 2.

3. The volume of an irregular solid cannot be determined in the same way as a rectangular solid, since length, width, and height cannot be accurately measured. However, the volume of an irregular solid can be measured by the displacement of water.

4. Place some water in the graduated cylinder and read its volume to the nearest 0.1 mL. Carefully add a sample of clay, making sure you do not let any water splash out of the graduated cylinder. Read the new volume to the nearest 0.1 mL. Subtract the original volume from the new volume. This volume of displaced water is equal to the volume of the clay sample. Record this value in Data Table 2.

5. Repeat the procedure for the other four samples of clay. Record your data in Data Table 2.

6. Using the mass and volume values in Data Table 2, construct a graph that illustrates the relationship between mass and volume of each sample. Use the vertical axis for mass and the horizontal axis for volume.

7. Connect the five points on the graph and extend the line to the zero point. The line should be a straight one connecting as many points as possible.

Observations
Part A

DATA TABLE 1

Description of Object	Material (if Known)	Mass (g)	Volume (cm³)	Density (g/cm³)
Bar	Iron Copper Aluminum			
Cube	Iron Copper Aluminum			

Part B

DATA TABLE 2

Clay	Mass (g)	Volume (cm³)
Sample 1		
Sample 2		
Sample 3		
Sample 4		
Sample 5		

Analysis and Conclusions

1. How do the densities of your two samples compare? Explain your observation.

_____

_____

_____

_____

2. What is the volume of a solid whose dimensions are 1.0 cm × 6.0 cm × 2.0 cm?

Remember to include the proper units. _____

_____

3. If the mass of the object in question 2 is 60 g, what is its density?

_____

_____

4. Using your graph, determine the volume of a sample of clay that has a mass of 160 g.

_____

5. Using your graph, determine the density of a piece of clay that has a volume of 3 cm³.

_____ g/cm³

6. Using your graph (or data from your data table), determine the density of a piece of clay

that has a mass of 25 g. _____ g/cm³

GRAPH

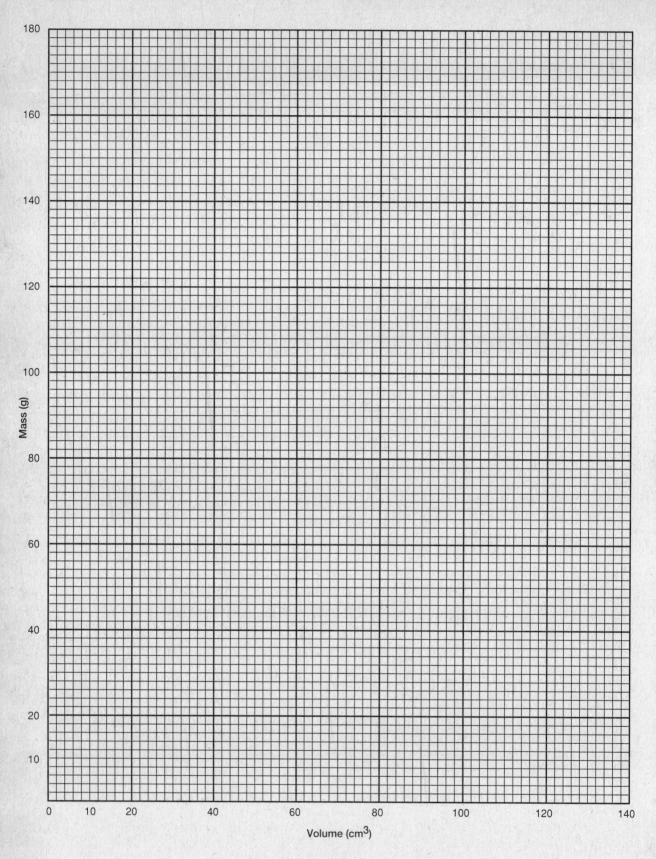

Critical Thinking and Application

1. Could the water displacement method be used to determine the volume of a rectangular

   solid as well as an irregular solid? _____ Explain. _____

   _____

   _____

2. If an object with a density of 5g/cm³ is cut into two equal pieces, what is the density of
   each piece?

   _____

3. The diagrams below represent three samples of the same substance, each having a
   different size and shape. Arrange the letters of the samples to show the order by volume

   from largest to smallest. _____

   What is the density of A?   B?   C?

   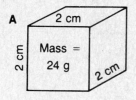
   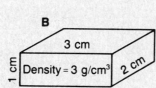
   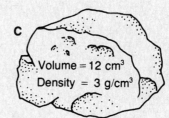

4. Explain how the results of this laboratory investigation show that differences in size and
   shape do not affect the density of a given substance.

   _____

   _____

   _____

5. Why is density such an important physical property?

   _____

   _____

   _____

   _____

   _____

Going Further

1. The density of water is 1 g/cm^3. An object will float in water if its density is less than 1 g/cm^3. If its density is greater than 1 g/cm^3, the object will sink. Given the following substances and their densities, determine whether each substance will float or sink in water.

aluminum 2.7 g/cm^3 ____   gold   19.3 g/cm^3 ____   chlorine   3.2 g/cm^3 ____

arsenic   5.7 g/cm^3 ____   neon   0.89 g/cm^3 ____   uranium 19.0 g/cm^3 ____

helium   0.18 g/cm^3 ____   lithium 0.53 g/cm^3 ____   potassium 0.86 g/cm^3 ____

2. Substance X has a volume of 50 cm^3 and a mass of 160 g. Will substance X float or sink?

_____

Substance Y has a volume of 140 cm^3 and a mass of 112 g. Will substance Y float or sink?

_____

_____ *Laboratory Investigation* _____

Chapter 2   General Properties of Matter
                                                    4 _____

Determining the Density of Liquids

Background Information

In the text you learned that mass and volume are general properties of all matter. Density is the ratio of mass to volume. The particular density of a specific kind of matter helps to identify it and distinguish it from other kinds of matter. Liquids have density, and it is possible to determine their densities in grams per milliliter (g/mL).

In this investigation you will determine the density of several liquids by measuring their mass and volume. You will also learn how to calculate the density of liquids by using a wood float.

Problem

How can you determine the density of liquids?

Materials *(per group)*

4 100-mL graduated cylinders
wooden cylinder about 10 cm
   long (A small pencil or thin
   dowel works well.)
laboratory balance
50 mL ethyl alcohol

oil (salad type)
salt water (several samples of
   different concentrations—
   A, B, C)
wax marking pencil

Procedure

1. Place the empty graduated cylinder on the laboratory balance. Record the mass in the Data Table.

2. Pour 50 mL of water into the graduated cylinder. Find the mass of the graduated cylinder and the water. Record this mass in the Data Table. Calculate the mass of the water by subtracting the mass of the empty graduated cylinder from the mass of the graduated cylinder with water. Record your answer in the Data Table. Keep the water in the cylinder for use in step 5.

3. Calculate the density of water by dividing the mass of the water by the volume.

$$\text{Density} = \frac{\text{Mass}}{\text{Volume}}$$

4. Using three other graduated cylinders, repeat steps 2 and 3 first using alcohol, then one of the samples of salt water, and then oil. Keep the liquids in the cylinders for use in step 5.

5. Carefully place the wooden cylinder in each liquid in the graduated cylinders, one at a time. See Figure 1. Note the level of the wooden cylinder in the water, the alcohol, the salt water, and the oil. In which liquid does the wooden cylinder float highest? In which liquid does the wooden cylinder float lowest?

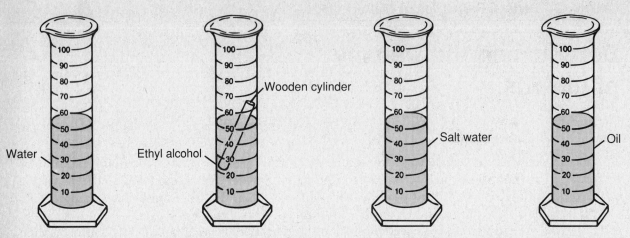

Figure 1

6. Use the wooden cylinder to test the remaining samples of salt water. With a wax marking pencil, mark the float levels of the salt water on your wooden cylinder.

Observations

DATA TABLE

Liquid	Mass of Empty Graduate (g)	Mass of Graduate and Liquid (g)	Mass of Liquid (g)	Volume of Liquid (mL)	Density of Liquid (g/mL)
Water				50	
Alcohol				50	
Salt water				50	
Oil				50	

Analysis and Conclusions

1. Which sample of salt water was the most dense? How did you know?

_____

_____

_____

2. List the four liquids you used in this experiment in order of increasing density.

_____

_____

Critical Thinking and Application

1. Which has the greater mass, 1 L of water or 1 L of alcohol? Why?

_____

2. Which takes up a greater volume, 1000 g of water or 1000 g of alcohol? Why?

_____

_____

_____

3. Which is more dense, 1 mL of water or 50 L of water? Why?

_____

_____

4. Predict what would happen if all the liquids used in this lab were poured into one beaker.

_____

_____

_____

_____

Going Further

Determine the density of each sample of salt water used in this investigation. Describe the method you used. Construct a table of your results.

Name _____ Class _____ Date _____

_____ *Laboratory Investigation* _____

Determining Specific Gravity

Background Information

One of the physical properties of matter that may be used to identify it is its specific gravity. Specific gravity is a comparison between the density of a substance and the density of pure water. Since the density of pure water is 1.0 g/mL, a substance with a specific gravity of 3.5, for example, would be 3.5 times denser than water.

In this investigation you will determine the specific gravity of several different substances by finding the mass of each and comparing it to the mass of the same volume of water.

Problem

How can an object's specific gravity be determined?

Materials *(per student or per group)*

mineral sample
rock sample
rubber stopper
cork
triple-beam balance
overflow can
250-mL beaker

Procedure

1. Find the mass of the empty, dry beaker. Record the mass in the Data Table.

2. Find the mass of the first object. Record the mass in the Data Table.

3. Fill the overflow can with water so that the water is above the spout. Allow the excess water to spill out into the sink.

4. Carefully drop the object into the overflow can and catch the displaced water in the beaker. If the object floats, push it down with a pencil or pen so that it is completely under water.

5. Find the mass of the beaker plus the water. Calculate the mass of the water alone and record it in the Data Table.

6. Calculate the specific gravity of the object according to the following ratio:

$$\text{Specific gravity} = \frac{\text{Mass of object}}{\text{Mass of displaced water}}$$

7. Repeat steps 1 through 6 for each additional object.

Observations

DATA TABLE

Object	Mass of Beaker	Mass of Water and Beaker	Mass of Displaced Water	Mass of Object	Specific Gravity

Analysis and Conclusions

1. When the object is placed in the overflow can, it displaces a certain volume of water. How does the volume of displaced water compare to the volume of the object?

_____

_____

2. What is the relationship between specific gravity and density?

_____

_____

_____

3. If the object floats in water, why is it necessary to submerge it to obtain accurate results? _____

_____

_____

_____

Critical Thinking and Application

1. Explain why the specific gravity of certain objects, such as table salt, cannot be determined by the method used in this investigation.

_____

_____

_____

_____

2. If two objects have the same specific gravity, does it mean that they are made of the same

kind of matter? Explain. _____

_____

_____

_____

3. How could you use specific gravity to help you find out if a piece of gold jewelry is made

of real gold or some other substance? _____

_____

_____

_____

_____

_____

_____

Going Further

This is not the only method of finding specific gravity. Use reference books to find out
about other methods that may be used to determine specific gravity.

_____ *Laboratory Investigation* _____

Investigating Phase Changes

Background Information

Pure matter can exist in three phases: solid, liquid, and gas. A phase change occurs when matter changes from one phase to another. Phase changes occur when heat is added or removed from a substance. The melting point of a substance is the temperature at which the solid-liquid phase change takes place. The freezing point is the temperature at which the liquid-solid phase change takes place. Notice that the melting point of a substance is the same as its freezing point. At this temperature, solid and liquid can exist together.

In Part A of this investigation you will observe what happens when the compound paradichlorobenzene (PDB) is cooled from a liquid to a solid, or freezes. In Part B the procedure will be reversed, and the solid will be heated until the substance melts and reaches a temperature above its melting point. The data obtained from Parts A and B will be used to construct a graph.

Problem

What temperature changes occur when a substance changes phase?

Materials *(per group)*

4 g paradichlorobenzene crystals
test tube
Celsius thermometer
hot plate
test-tube holder or clamp
2 400-mL beakers
safety goggles
heat-resistant gloves
test-tube rack
colored pencils
glass-marking pencil

Procedure
Part A

1. Half fill the two beakers with water. Heat one of the beakers on the hot plate until the temperature of the water is about 90°C. Do not boil the water.

2. Obtain a test tube of PDB crystals and place it in the beaker of hot water. Allow the PDB to melt completely. As soon as it is melted, insert a thermometer in it and record the temperature. See Figure 1.

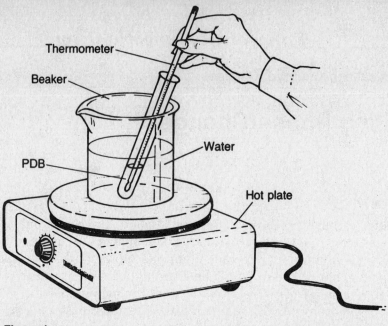

Thermometer

Beaker

PDB

Water

Hot plate

Figure 1

3. Remove the test tube from the beaker and place it in the beaker of cool water. Hold the thermometer in the PDB so that it does not touch the sides of the test tube, and record the temperature every 30 seconds in Data Table 1. Between readings, stir the PDB constantly until it becomes solid. Be sure to note in your data when the liquid PDB first starts to solidify and when there is no liquid PDB left. Continue to record the temperature until it drops to 40°C.

4. Note what happens to the volume of liquid PDB as it turns into solid PDB.

Part B

5. Be sure the beaker of water on the hot plate is still heated as in step 1. Place the test tube with solid PDB in the beaker of hot water. Record the temperature of PDB in Data Table 2 as soon as you place it in the hot water. Read and record the temperature every 30 seconds until solid PDB has changed completely to liquid.

6. When the thermometer is able to move, use it to stir the mixture of solid-liquid PDB. Continue stirring and recording the temperature every 30 seconds until the temperature of the sample reaches 60°C. Note in your data when the solid PDB begins to melt and when it has completely melted.

7. Remove the thermometer and wipe it clean. Remove the test tube from the hot water and allow it to cool in the test-tube rack before replacing the cork and returning it to your teacher.

8. Graph your data on Graph 1. Use one color for the data you obtained while cooling the PDB and another color for the data you obtained while heating the PDB. Provide a key to indicate what each color represents.

Observations

DATA TABLE 1 (Cooling Curve)

Time (min)	Temperature (°C)	Time (min)	Temperature (°C)
½		7½	
1		8	
1½		8½	
2		9	
2½		9½	
3		10	
3½		10½	
4		11	
4½		11½	
5		12	
5½		12½	
6		13	
6½		13½	
7		14	

DATA TABLE 2 (Heating Curve)

Time (min)	Temperature (°C)	Time (min)	Temperature (°C)
½		7½	
1		8	
1½		8½	
2		9	
2½		9½	
3		10	
3½		10½	
4		11	
4½		11½	
5		12	
5½		12½	
6		13	
6½		13½	
7		14	

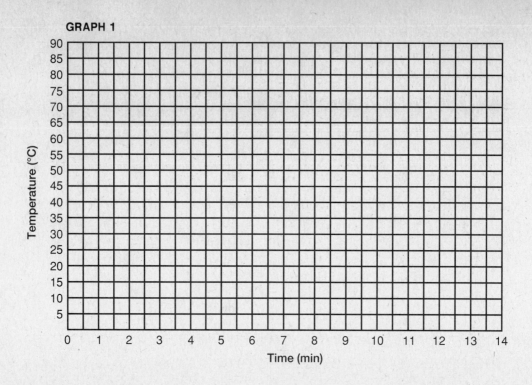

GRAPH 1

Temperature (°C) vs. Time (min)

Analysis and Conclusions

1. At what temperature does PDB become solid? _____ How does this compare to the temperature at which solid PDB become a liquid? _____

_____

2. Looking at the slopes of the lines on your graph, how many different sections make up your graph? _____

3. Describe what occurs in the section on your graph where the line is horizontal.

_____

_____

_____

_____

4. What happened to the volume of PDB as it became a solid?

_____

What does this indicate about the density of solid PDB as compared to liquid PDB?

_____

_____

_____

Critical Thinking and Application

1. As the PDB was melting, heat was being added to it but the temperature did not rise.

Where did the heat energy go? _____

_____

2. If you used ice instead of PDB in this experiment, how do you think your results would

be different? _____

_____

_____

_____

_____

_____

3. If you used twice as much PDB, how would your results be different? Explain.

_____

_____

_____

_____

_____

_____

4. A student wanted to solve the problem: "Which freezes fastest, hot water or cold water?"
Using the scientific method, describe an experiment the student might do to find the

answer. _____

_____

_____

_____

_____

_____

What would your hypothesis be if you were doing this experiment?

_____

_____

_____

_____

Going Further

Do the experiment you have described in answer to question 4. Record your observations and conclusions.

_____ *Laboratory Investigation* _____

7

Physical and Chemical Changes

Background Information

Matter is constantly changing. The two kinds of changes that occur in matter are physical and chemical changes. In a physical change, no new substances are formed. However, physical properties such as size, shape, color, or phase may change. Dissolving, melting, evaporating, and grinding are examples of physical change.

As a result of chemical change, one or more "new" substances with new and different properties are formed. The new substances are different from the original substance. Burning and the rusting of iron are examples of chemical change.

In this investigation you will observe physical and chemical changes and learn to recognize each type of change when it occurs.

Problem

What are the differences between physical and chemical changes?

Materials (*per student*)

birthday candle
aluminum foil (15 cm × 15 cm)
modeling clay
small piece of paper
watch glass
Bunsen burner
scoop
magnesium ribbon (1 cm long)
1 M hydrochloric acid
safety goggles
2 test tubes
test-tube rack
test-tube clamp
insulating pad
matches
table salt
dropper bottle of 0.1 M silver
  nitrate

Procedure

1. Take a small piece of modeling clay and place it on the square of aluminum foil. Firmly place a candle in the clay so that it is well supported. Light the candle and allow it to burn while you continue with the rest of the investigation. Record your observations of the burning candle in the space provided in Observations.

2. Tear the piece of paper into small pieces and place them on the watch glass. Place the watch glass and pieces of paper on the insulating pad. Light the pieces of paper with a match and allow them to burn completely. Record your observations of the burning paper.

3. Add a small scoop of table salt to a test tube that has been half-filled with tap water. Place your thumb over the top of the test tube and shake to dissolve the salt. Record your observations. Using the dropper, add 5 drops of silver nitrate to the salt water. Record your observations.

4. Place a small piece of magnesium ribbon in a test tube. Add 5 drops of hydrochloric acid to the test tube. Touch the bottom of the test tube with your fingertips. Record your observations.

Observations

1. What did you observe as the candle burned? _____

_____

_____

What was left after the candle burned? _____

_____

2. What did you observe as the paper burned? _____

_____

What was left after the paper burned? _____

_____

3. What did you observe when you added the salt to the water in the test tube and shook it? _____

_____

What did you observe when the silver nitrate was added to the salt water?

_____

_____

4. What did you observe when the hydrochloric acid was added to the magnesium metal?

_____

_____

_____

_____

Analysis and Conclusions

1. Identify each of the following as either a physical change or chemical change. Give a reason for your answer.

   a. Melting candle wax _____
   _____

   b. Burning a candle _____
   _____

   c. Tearing paper _____
   _____

   d. Burning paper _____
   _____

   e. Dissolving table salt _____
   _____

   f. Mixing salt water and silver nitrate _____
   _____

   g. Cutting a piece of magnesium ribbon _____
   _____

   h. Adding hydrochloric acid to magnesium metal _____
   _____

2. Describe two observations you might make when a physical change occurs.
   _____
   _____
   _____

3. Describe two observations you might make when a chemical change occurs.
   _____
   _____
   _____

Critical Thinking and Application

1. How could you show that dissolving the salt in water resulted in a physical change?

_____

_____

_____

2. How could you show that adding acid to the magnesium ribbon resulted in a chemical

change? _____

_____

_____

_____

3. The following changes can sometimes indicate that a chemical change has occurred. Explain how each change might result from a physical, not a chemical, change.

a. Change of color _____

_____

b. Loss of mass _____

_____

c. The substance seems to "disappear." _____

_____

_____

_____

Going Further

Write out a recipe that involves cooking or baking. Identify each step in the recipe as resulting in either a physical change or a chemical change in the ingredients.

_____ *Laboratory Investigation* _____

Determining Solubility

Background Information

Several factors affect the rate at which solids dissolve in liquids. These factors include the nature of the solute and solvent, the temperature, and the degree of fineness to which the solute has been ground. There is no general rule to predict how much solute will dissolve in a given solvent, but you can determine the effect certain variables have on the rate of solution.

In this investigation you will determine the amount of potassium nitrate that can be dissolved in 10 mL of water at a given temperature.

Problem

How can you determine the solubility of a substance in water?

Materials *(per group)*

weighing paper
25 mL potassium nitrate
water
100-mL graduated cylinder
250-mL beaker
Celsius thermometer
Bunsen burner
2 test tubes
laboratory balance
1 test-tube holder
ice
glass stirring rod
safety goggles

Procedure

1. Place a small sheet of plain paper on the laboratory balance. Record the mass of the paper. Adjust the balance so that it registers 25 g more than the mass of the paper alone.

2. Slowly and carefully add potassium nitrate to the paper until the balance is again level. In this way, you have poured out 25 g of potassium nitrate.

3. Pour 10 mL of water into one test tube. Warm the test tube over the Bunsen burner until the first temperature assigned to you by your teacher is reached. Try to maintain this temperature throughout the next step.

4. Pour a small amount of potassium nitrate into the test tube. Stir carefully. If the potassium nitrate dissolves completely, add a little more. Continue until no more dissolves and a few small grains settle to the bottom of the test tube.

5. Record the exact temperature of the solution.

6. Find the mass of the paper and the remaining potassium nitrate again. Determine the amount of potassium nitrate you used by subtracting this amount from the original mass.

7. Repeat the procedure with another 10 mL of water. However, this time cool the water in ice until the second temperature assigned to you by your teacher is reached. Again determine the amount of potassium nitrate that dissolves in the water. Record the exact temperature.

8. Report your information to your teacher. He or she will compile all the information obtained by the class. In this way, you will find out how much potassium nitrate dissolves in 10 mL of water over a wide temperature range.

9. Graph your results and the results of your classmates in Graph 1.

Observations

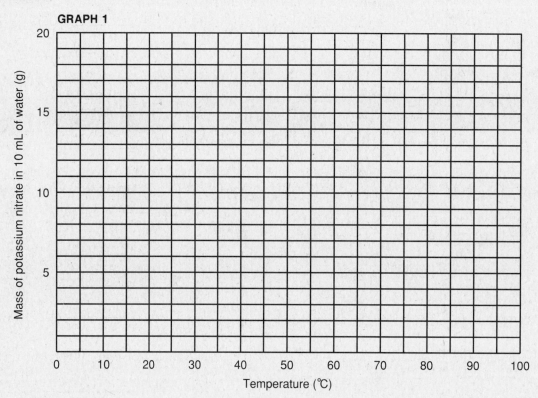

GRAPH 1

Analysis and Conclusions

1. What effect does temperature have on the amount of potassium nitrate that can be

dissolved in a given amount of water? _____

_____

_____

2. From the graph, predict how much potassium nitrate would dissolve in 10 mL of water at

60°C. _____

3. How much potassium nitrate do you think would dissolve in 100 mL of water at 60°C?

_____

4. To what temperature would 10 mL of water have to be heated to completely dissolve

14 g of potassium nitrate? _____

Critical Thinking and Application

1. If the temperature of a saturated solution of potassium nitrate were to drop, what would

you notice? _____

_____

2. If 10 mL of a saturated solution of potassium nitrate were to cool from 60°C to 10°C,
how much potassium nitrate would be found on the bottom of the test tube?

_____

3. Suppose you had measured the solubility of KNO_3 only at 10°C and 90°C. How might

your solubility graph be inaccurate? _____

_____

_____

_____

4. Based on the graph, how much KNO_3 do you think would dissolve in 10 mL of water at

100°C? _____

Going Further

Determine the solubility graph for sodium chloride (table salt). How does this graph
differ from the graph for potassium nitrate?

_____ *Laboratory Investigation* _____

Chapter 4   Mixtures, Elements, and Compounds _____ **9** ____

Relating Solubility and Temperature

Background Information

The solubility of a substance indicates how much of that substance will dissolve in a given volume of water. The substance being dissolved is called the solute. The substance that does the dissolving is called the solvent. And the resulting substance is called the solution. So solubility tells you how much solute dissolves in a solvent. Solubility depends upon the nature of the solvent, the nature of the solute, and the temperature of the solution. In this investigation you will determine the effect of temperature on the solution process.

Problem

How does the temperature of a solution affect a solute's ability to dissolve?

Materials *(per group)*

ring stand and ring
wire gauze
400-mL beaker
Bunsen burner
4 medium-sized test tubes
    labeled A, B, C, D
triple-beam balance
30 grams of
    potassium nitrate (KNO_3)
100-mL graduated cylinder
stirring rod
test-tube rack
Celsius thermometer
tongs
graph paper
safety goggles
heat-resistant gloves

Procedure

🧪🔥 1. Assemble a ring stand, wire gauze, Bunsen burner, and beaker as shown in Figure 1. Fill the beaker approximately half full of water and begin heating the water. Do not boil the water; just heat it to between 80° and 90°C. Use the thermometer to measure the water temperature, and turn off the burner once the water reaches the desired temperature range.

🧰 2. **CAUTION:** *In this part of the procedure, use extreme care in handling potassium nitrate. Do not allow it to come in contact with your skin.* Use the balance to measure a sample of potassium nitrate with a mass of 11 g. Place this sample in test tube A. Measure another sample with a mass of 8 g and place it in test tube B. Continue this procedure, measuring 6 g for test tube C and 4 g for test tube D.

Figure 1

🧪 3. Now add exactly 10 mL of water to each test tube.

4. Put the four labeled test tubes with their contents into the hot water in the beaker. Using a stirring rod, carefully stir the contents of each test tube to make sure all of the KNO_3 dissolves.

🖐️ 5. Allow the test tubes to remain in the hot water for 5 minutes. All of the KNO_3 in each test tube should now be completely dissolved. Remove the test tubes from the beaker with tongs and place them in the test-tube rack to cool. **CAUTION:** *Exercise care in handling the hot test tubes.*

🧪 6. Now place the thermometer in test tube A and note the temperature at which you first notice the clear liquid becoming cloudy as crystals form in the solution. Record this temperature in the appropriate column in the Data Table.

7. Quickly wipe the thermometer off, place it in test tube B, and note the temperature at which you first notice the liquid becoming cloudy as crystals form in the solution. Record this temperature in the Data Table.

8. Repeat this procedure for the two remaining test tubes. Record your data.

Observations

DATA TABLE

Test Tube	Temperature at Which Solute Starts to Form Crystals	Grams of KNO_3 per 10 mL Water	Calculated Grams of KNO_3 per 100 mL Water
A		11	
B		8	
C		6	
D		4	

Analysis and Conclusions

1. If 11 g of KNO_3 were dissolved in 10 mL of water in test tube A, how many grams of KNO_3 would have to be dissolved in 100 mL of water to give the same

   proportion? _____ How many grams in test tube B? _____ In test tube C? _____ In

   test tube D? _____ Record these answers in the appropriate column of the Data Table.

2. Prepare a graph of your data. Use the vertical axis for grams of KNO_3 per 100 mL of water and the horizontal axis for temperature. Your graph should have a total of four experimental points.

3. Connect your data points with a solid line. Then use a dotted line to extend the smooth line to 0°C. The line you have just drawn is called a solubility curve. It can be used to determine the solubility of KNO_3 at any given temperature. According to your curve,

   what is the solubility in g/100 mL of water of KNO_3 at 0°C? _____

4. What can you say about the shape of the solubility curve for KNO_3?

   _____

5. At 20°C, the accepted value for the solubility of KNO_3 is 30 g/100 mL of water. How does this compare with the value derived from your graph?

   _____

   _____

Critical Thinking and Application

1. This type of experiment can be used to determine the solubility of many different solutes. Name two ways in which the solubility curve for carbon dioxide gas in water would differ from the one you drew for KNO_3.

   _____

   _____

2. Solubility depends upon three factors: the nature of the solvent, the nature of the solute, and the temperature of the solution. Which factor was the variable in this investigation?

   Which factors were held constant? _____

   _____

3. Suppose you wanted to test the solubility of KNO_3 in various solvents. How might you go

   about doing this? _____

   _____

   _____

4. A microbiologist wishes to prepare a solution of 650 g of KNO_3 in 1 L of water. Can she

prepare this solution at room temperature? _____

Explain your answer. _____

_____

_____

_____

Going Further

Figure 2 shows the solubility curves for several different solutes. Using the graph, answer the following questions.

1. How many grams of KCl will dissolve in 100 mL of water at 80°C? _____

2. What two substances show a decrease in solubility as the temperature increases?

_____

3. At what temperature are the solubilities of KCl and NaCl the same? _____

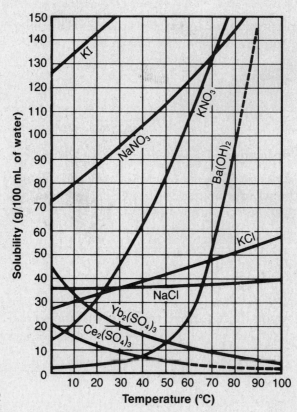

Figure 2

4. At a temperature of 80°C, 100 g of $Ba(OH)_2$ are completely dissolved in 100 mL of water. If the solution is cooled to about 62°C, how many grams come out of solution

because they can no longer be dissolved? _____

5. At 10°C, what substance has the greatest solubility in 100 mL of water? _____

_____ *Laboratory Investigation* _____

_____ **10** ____

Elements, Mixtures, and Compounds

Background Information

When two elements are combined, a chemical reaction does not always occur between them. Instead, the two elements form a mixture in which the properties of the two elements are retained.

When a chemical reaction does take place, the two elements form a compound. The compound has physical and chemical properties that the individual elements alone do not have.

The two elements in a mixture can be separated on the basis of differences in their physical properties. The two elements in a compound, however, can only be separated as a result of another chemical reaction.

In this investigation you will observe how physical and chemical properties are affected when two elements are combined.

Problem

How do the properties of elements differ in mixtures and in compounds?

Materials *(per group)*

triple-beam balance	sulfur powder	250-mL beaker
forceps	iron powder	magnet
scoop	hand lens	safety goggles
Bunsen burner	test tube	
matches	test-tube clamp	

Procedure

1. On your triple-beam balance, measure out 3 g of sulfur powder on a piece of paper.

2. Using the hand lens, observe the color of the sulfur and the size and shape of the particles. Record your observations in the Data Table.

3. Lift the edge of the paper containing the sulfur, place the magnet underneath, and move the magnet to see if it has any effect on the sulfur. Record your observations in the Data Table.

4. On your triple-beam balance, measure out 5 g of iron powder on a piece of paper.

5. Using the hand lens, observe the color of the iron powder and the size and shape of the particles. Record your observations in the Data Table.

6. Lift the edge of the paper containing the sulfur, place the magnet underneath, and move the magnet to see if it has any effect on the sulfur. Record your observations in the Data Table.

7. Mix the iron and sulfur together on one piece of paper. Use the scoop to make sure the mixture is uniform throughout. Repeat step 2 for the mixture. Record your observations in the Data Table.

8. Repeat step 3 for the mixture. Record your observations in the Data Table.

9. Half-fill the beaker with cold water and set it aside. Carefully place the iron-sulfur mixture in a test tube. Light the Bunsen burner. Holding the test tube with the test-tube clamp, heat the iron-sulfur mixture for about 5 minutes. **CAUTION:** *Make sure that the mouth of the test tube is pointed away from you and others.* Move the test tube around in the flame so that all of the contents are evenly heated. Record your observations in the Data Table.

Figure 1

10. When you see no further changes occurring in the test tube, shut off the Bunsen burner and immediately put the test tube into the beaker of cold water. If the test tube does not break, wrap it in several layers of paper towel and hit it with a hammer to crack the glass.

11. Using the forceps, hand lens, and magnet, examine the substance formed in the test tube. Record your observations in the Data Table.

Observations

DATA TABLE

Physical Properties	Sulfur	Iron	Iron-Sulfur Before Heating	Iron-Sulfur After Heating
Color				
Shape of particle				
Size of particle				
Effect of magnet				

What did you observe when you began heating the test tube containing the mixture of sulfur and iron? _____

_____

_____

Analysis and Conclusions

1. How did the properties of sulfur alone compare with the sulfur in the unheated iron-sulfur combination? _____

   _____

2. How did the properties of iron alone compare with the iron in the unheated iron-sulfur combination? _____

   _____

3. How did the properties of sulfur alone compare with the iron-sulfur combination after it was heated? _____

   _____

4. How did the properties of iron alone compare with the iron-sulfur combination after it was heated? _____

   _____

   _____

5. What kind of substance was the iron-sulfur combination before heating?

   _____

6. What was the effect of heating the iron-sulfur combination?

   _____

7. What kind of substance was the iron-sulfur combination after heating?

   _____

Critical Thinking and Application

1. Explain how you know that mixing the iron and sulfur together on the paper results in a mixture of the two substances. _____

   _____

   _____

   _____

2. Explain how you know that heating the iron and sulfur together in the test tube results in a new compound composed of chemically combined iron and sulfur.

_____

_____

_____

3. Why was it necessary to heat the test tube in order for a chemical reaction to occur?

_____

_____

_____

4. The element sodium reacts explosively with water and the element chlorine is a yellowish-green poisonous gas. When chemically combined, sodium and chlorine form nonexplosive, nonpoisonous table salt. Explain how this can be.

_____

_____

5. Identify each of the following as an element, a mixture, or a compound.

a. aluminum foil _____

b. air _____

c. water _____

d. salt water _____

e. copper wire _____

f. steel _____

Going Further

The chemical combination of iron and sulfur produces the compound iron sulfide, also known as the mineral pyrite. Consult reference sources to find the properties and uses of pyrite.

_____ *Laboratory Investigation* _____

11

Making Predictions Using Indirect Evidence

Background Information

How do scientists know what an atom looks like? After all, it is impossible to see an atom. Yet scientists have constructed models of an atom based on observations of how atoms behave. These observations are considered to be one type of indirect evidence for the structure of an atom.

Another type of indirect evidence comes from making predictions. Based on the model they have developed, scientists predict how atoms will behave in certain circumstances. They design experiments to test these predictions. If the predictions are shown to be accurate, they are taken as additional indirect evidence that the model is correct.

In this investigation you will use indirect evidence to determine the properties of an object you cannot see.

Problem

How can you determine the characteristics of something you cannot observe directly?

Materials *(per pair of students)*

shoe box, with cover, that
    contains small objects
laboratory balance

Procedure

1. Obtain a sealed shoe box from your instructor.

2. Without opening the box, perform several tests such as tipping it, shaking it, sliding it, and finding its mass. In each case, record your observations in the Data Table. In each case, the observation could be of a sound or of the way the object behaved (rolling, sliding, and so on). You might also wish to find the mass of an identical box and lid that is empty. The difference in mass would be the mass of the object or objects inside.

3. On the basis of your observations, sketch the object or objects in Drawing 1. Include any other characteristics, such as mass.

Observations

Describe some of the ways you tested the unknown objects to determine their characteristics. Record your descriptions in the Data Table.

DATA TABLE

Test	Observations

Analysis and Conclusions

DRAWING 1

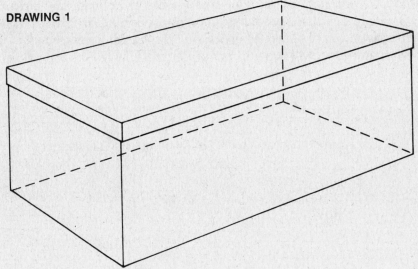

1. What senses did you use to determine a model of the object inside the box?

_____

_____

_____

2. How does this kind of activity compare with the way scientists have learned about the

atom? _____

_____

_____

_____

Critical Thinking and Application

1. In what ways could you test your model of the contents of the box?

   _____

   _____

   _____

2. What kinds of special instruments could also be used to make indirect observations of the

   contents of the box? _____

   _____

3. If you used some of the special instruments you mentioned and the results did not agree
   with your previous determination of the contents of the box, what would you need to

   do? _____

   _____

   _____

   _____

4. Open the box and directly observe the object(s) inside. How does your observation

   compare with your indirect determination? _____

   _____

   _____

   _____

   What does this tell you about the current model? _____

   _____

   _____

   _____

   _____

   _____

   _____

Going Further

1. Glue an object inside a shoe box. Trade boxes with another student who has done the same. Using knitting needles, determine the location and shape of the object by sticking the needles through the box.

2. How would you determine what kind of liquid was inside of a full, closed, opaque bottle? How would it be helpful if you had an identical empty bottle?

_____ *Laboratory Investigation* _____

Investigating Rutherford's Model of the Atom

Background Information

In 1911, Ernest Rutherford discovered that most of the atom is empty space. Almost all of the atom's mass is concentrated in an extremely small volume called the nucleus. The nucleus is located in the center of the atom. Rutherford discovered the existence of the nucleus in his famous scattering experiment. In this experiment, he aimed tiny, positively charged alpha particles at a very thin piece of gold foil. Rutherford observed that almost all the positively charged alpha particles passed through the gold foil with almost no deflection, or bending. This could only mean that the gold atoms in the sheet were mostly empty space!

However, Rutherford also observed that some particles were greatly deflected. In fact, a few bounced almost straight back from the gold foil. What could this mean? Rutherford knew that positive charges repel other positive charges. So he proposed that an atom had a small, positively charged center. He called this center the nucleus. In this investigation you will duplicate Rutherford's experiment.

Problem

How can the presence of an "invisible" charged particle be detected?

Materials *(per group)*

sheet of white paper,
    50 cm × 20 cm
pencil
metric ruler
target platform with "nucleus"
    and ramp attached
tape
sheet of colored paper,
    30 cm × 20 cm
2 strips of posterboard,
    30 cm × 2 cm
strip of posterboard,
    20 cm × 2 cm
"alpha particle"
flour

Procedure

Part A Constructing Your Setup

1. On the sheet of white paper, draw a series of lines lengthwise, 2 cm from each other. When you are finished there should be about ten parallel lines.

2. Tape this paper to the elevated ramp, as shown in Figure 1.

Figure 1

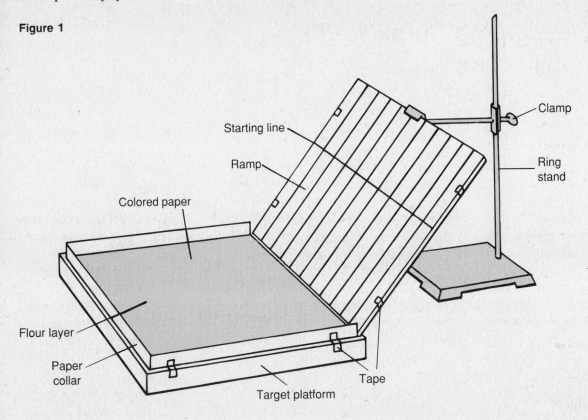

3. Tape the piece of colored paper to the target platform. **Note:** *Be sure that the edge of the paper does not interfere with the sliding of the "alpha particle" down the ramp to the platform.*

4. Place the alpha particle about halfway up the ramp. Make sure that the smooth surface of the alpha particle is facing down.

5. Allow the alpha particle to slide down the ramp and cross the platform. **Note:** *The alpha particle should not come to a stop until it is at least halfway across the target platform.* If it stops too soon, release it from a higher position on the ramp.

6. Adjust the height of the ramp until the alpha particle slides about 20 cm across the target platform before stopping. Using the ruler, draw a line across the ramp at this height.

7. Carefully sprinkle some flour on the platform so that the platform is entirely covered with flour. Use your ruler to create a smooth and even layer of flour. The flour will aid you in observing the path of the alpha particle.

Part B Duplicating Rutherford's Experiment

1. Release the alpha particle on the line on the ramp closest to you. Make sure that you position the alpha particle at your starting line.

2. Using the pencil, draw the exact path the alpha particle took in the flour on the colored paper. Label this line 1.

3. Smooth out the surface of the flour with your ruler.

4. Release the alpha particle along the next line. Draw its path on the colored paper. Label this line 2.

5. Repeat steps 2 and 3 until the alpha particle has been released from each of the vertical lines.

6. When you are finished, carefully remove the colored paper from the target platform. Carefully dispose of the flour.

Observations

1. On which areas of the target platform were the paths of the alpha particle straight

   lines? _____

2. How many lines were deflected, or bent, on the target platform?

   _____

   _____

3. From your observations, locate the target "nucleus" on your colored paper. Draw its approximate size and shape. Attach the colored paper to this laboratory investigation.

Analysis and Conclusions

1. If the target platform represents an atom, is the target nucleus the same size as the atom?

   Explain. _____

   _____

2. Did the target nucleus attract or repel the alpha particle? _____

   Explain. _____

   _____

Critical Thinking and Application

1. In Rutherford's actual experiment, electric forces deflected the positive alpha particles from the positive target nuclei. In your duplication of Rutherford's experiment, what type of force did you use to deflect the alpha particle? How could you prove that you

   used this type of force? _____

   _____

   _____

   _____

2. In Rutherford's actual experiments, nearly all the alpha particles passed straight through and were not deflected at all. What does this tell you about the size of the nucleus of an

atom? _____

_____

As a result of these experiments, of what does an atom seem to mostly consist?

_____

_____

3. In other experiments, Rutherford aimed beta particles, which are high-speed, negatively

charged electrons, at the foil and screen. Predict the behavior of the beta particles. _____

_____

_____

_____

4. Rutherford repeated these experiments using foils made of metals other than gold.

Predict the results of these experiments. _____

_____

_____

Going Further

Find out about the contributions made by Crookes, Thomson, and Millikan to the discovery of the electron.

_____ *Laboratory Investigation* _____

Relating Electrons
and Probability

Background Information

Early theories of the structure of the atom described the movement of electrons around the nucleus as similar to the movement of the planets around the sun. Today scientists know this is not the case. Electrons do not travel around the nucleus in fixed orbits. Electrons move in an area known as the electron cloud. The electron cloud is a region in which electrons are likely to be found. Within the electron cloud, electrons are arranged in energy levels. Energy levels represent the most probable location in which an electron can be found. An energy level should not be confused with a specific path. For electrons do not have a path. In fact, scientists can speak only of the chances, or probability, of finding electrons at various locations—not of their exact position. In this investigation you will get a better understanding of probability and how it relates to electrons.

Problem

How can the movement of electrons outside the nucleus be described?

Materials *(per group)*

1 die
masking tape
1 sheet of graph paper having
    1½ squares to the centimeter

Procedure

1. Prepare your die in the following way: Tape all six sides. Mark three of the sides with one dot each, two of the sides with two dots each, and the remaining side with three dots.

2. Select a square near the center of the graph paper and color it red. This red square will represent the nucleus.

3. Roll the die and with each roll pencil in a square according to the following rules.
   - If a one is rolled, pencil in any square that is between 0 and 3 cm from the nucleus.
   - If a two is rolled, pencil in any square that is between 3 and 5 cm from the nucleus.
   - If a three is rolled, pencil in any square that is between 5 and 7 cm from the nucleus.

4. Repeat this procedure of rolling the die and marking the graph for 50 throws. Record your results in the Data Table.

Observations

DATA TABLE	Number of Squares Penciled In
0–3 cm (first energy level)	
3–5 cm (second energy level)	
5–7 cm (third energy level)	

1. The modern view of the movement of electrons in an atom is based on the concept of probability. What is the definition of probability? _____

_____

_____

_____

2. In which range do you have the most darkened squares on your diagram?

_____

_____

3. Compare your diagram to that of a classmate. Are they identical?

_____

_____

In what ways are they alike? Different? _____

_____

_____

_____

Analysis and Conclusions

1. Based on your data, in what energy level is an electron most likely to be found?

_____ Least likely to be found? _____

72

2. If each square that you penciled in represents a chance of finding an electron in a particular location around the nucleus, where would you look first for an electron?

Explain your answer. _____

_____

_____

3. Can the exact position of an electron around the nucleus be determined?

_____

What can be known about electrons? _____

_____

Critical Thinking and Application

1. Mathematically, the probability of an event occurring is equal to the number of favorable outcomes divided by the number of possible outcomes. According to the way you marked your die at the beginning of this investigation, what is the probability of an electron being found in the first energy level? The second? The third?

_____

_____

2. Suppose you had rolled the die 100 times. How do you think your results would have compared with the results you obtained by rolling the die 50 times?

_____

_____

_____

_____

3. Suppose you wanted to determine the probability of a student being found at various locations in your school building at 10 AM. How might you investigate this problem?

_____

_____

_____

_____

_____

_____

Going Further

Each energy level in an atom can hold only a certain number of electrons. The first energy level, closest to the nucleus, can hold at most 2 electrons. For the elements in the chart, the second and third energy levels are considered full when they have 8 electrons each. Using this information, fill in the chart below.

Element	Number of Electrons	Electron Arrangement			
		First Energy Level	Second Energy Level	Third Energy Level	Fourth Energy Level
Hydrogen					
Helium					
Carbon					
Oxygen					
Neon					
Sodium					
Aluminum					
Sulfur					
Chlorine					
Calcium					

Laboratory Investigation

14

The Alkaline Earth Elements

Background Information

The arrangement of the elements in the periodic table is one of the most important achievements in modern chemistry. The physical and chemical properties of elements change in a regular pattern as you go both across the rows and down the columns of the periodic table. As a result, when elements close to each other in a row or column are compared, they have many of the same properties. However, when elements farther away from each other in a row or column are compared, they have more dissimilar properties.

The elements in Group 2 of the periodic table are known as the alkaline earth elements. Like all members of a group, or family, of elements, they have certain properties that change in a regular pattern within the group. One of these properties is the ability to form a precipitate, or solid substance, as a result of a chemical reaction. The precipitate cannot dissolve in water and eventually settles to the bottom of the container.

In this investigation you will compare the abilities of the alkaline earth elements to form precipitates as a result of a chemical reaction.

Materials *(per group)*

safety goggles
spot plate
sheet of notebook paper
dropper bottles of:
    magnesium nitrate
    calcium nitrate
    strontium nitrate
    barium nitrate
    potassium carbonate
    potassium sulfate
    potassium chromate

Procedure

1. Place the spot plate in the center of a sheet of notebook paper so that there are 4 spots running down and 3 spots running across. See Figure 1.

2. Along the side of the notebook paper next to each of the four spots, write the names of the four alkaline earth elements that are present in each nitrate compound listed in the materials you are using. Write them in the same order in which they are listed. See Figure 1.

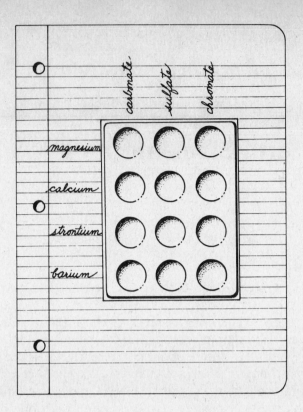

Figure 1

3. Along the top of the notebook paper next to each of the three spots, write the names of the three substances that are combined with potassium in the materials you are using. See Figure 1.

4. Put on your safety goggles. Place 3 drops of potassium carbonate in each of the four spots under the word Carbonate. Place 3 drops of potassium sulfate in each of the four spots under the word Sulfate. Place 3 drops of potassium chromate in each of the four spots under the word Chromate. Be very careful not to mix the liquid from one spot with the liquid from another.

5. Take the dropper bottle of magnesium nitrate and place 3 drops in each of the three spots in the row labeled Magnesium. Observe each spot carefully and record the result in the Data Table. Repeat this procedure using the dropper bottles containing calcium nitrate, strontium nitrate, and barium nitrate. Be very careful not to mix the liquid from one spot with the liquid from another.

6. After recording your results, wash your spot plate thoroughly with soapy water and a brush.

Observations

DATA TABLE

Alkaline Earth Metal	Carbonate	Sulfate	Chromate
Magnesium			
Calcium			
Strontium			
Barium			

76

Analysis and Conclusions

1. Was there evidence of a chemical reaction occurring in any of the spots? _____

   Explain your answer. _____

   _____

   _____

2. Which alkaline earth element formed the smallest number of precipitates? _____

3. Which alkaline earth element formed the greatest number of precipitates? _____

4. What is the relationship between the number of precipitates formed and the location of

   the alkaline earth element on the periodic table? _____

   _____

   _____

5. If the ability of an alkaline earth element to form a precipitate is an indication of its
   ability to chemically react with other substances, which is the most reactive element?

   _____

   The least reactive?

   _____

6. List the alkaline earth metals in order of their chemical reactivity, starting with the most

   reactive. _____

   _____

7. How does the order of the elements you listed in question 6 compare to their order in

   the periodic table? _____

   _____

Critical Thinking and Application

1. Why were you cautioned not to mix the solution in one spot with the solution in another

   spot on your spot plate? _____

   _____

2. Group 1 in the periodic table is known as the alkali metals. Based on your investigation of the Group 2 elements, predict the comparative reactivity of the elements in Group 1 of the periodic table.

_____

3. If you had a solution containing a mixture of magnesium, strontium, and barium, how could you separate the three elements?
Hint: Review the information in the Data Table.

_____

_____

_____

Going Further

Perform the procedure you described in your answer to question 3. Be sure to check the procedure with your teacher before starting. Describe your investigation in a laboratory report that includes title, problem, materials, procedure, observations, and conclusions.

_____ *Laboratory Investigation* _____

15

Investigating the Activity Series of the Metals

Background Information

One way to arrange the elements in the periodic table is by order of their activity. A metal is said to be more active than another metal if it will replace the less active metal from a solution of one of its compounds. This can be observed because the metal with the lower activity is "plated out" as pure metal on the piece of metal with the higher activity. By performing a series of experiments, you can develop a list of metals in order of their activity.

In this investigation you will test zinc, copper, and lead to see if they will replace each other in solutions of their compounds. Using your results, you can develop a short list in order of activity.

Problem

How can you determine the relative activities of zinc, copper, and lead?

Materials *(per pair of students)*

solutions
    copper sulfate
    lead acetate
    zinc sulfate
10-cm strips
    zinc
    lead
    copper
sandpaper
9 small test tubes
test-tube rack
safety goggles
masking tape

Procedure

👁 **1.** Put on safety goggles.

2. Arrange the nine test tubes in three groups of three each. Using small pieces of masking tape, label the first three test tubes Lead Acetate, the next three Zinc Sulfate, and the last three Copper Sulfate. See Figure 1.

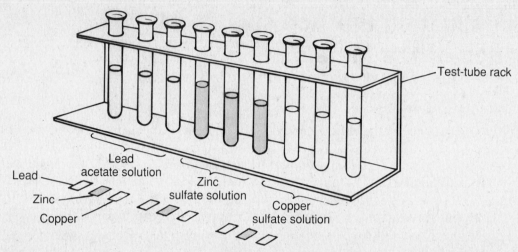

Figure 1

🔺 **3.** Fill the appropriately labeled three tubes one third full of lead acetate solution. Fill the appropriately labeled three tubes one third full of zinc sulfate solution. Fill the appropriately labeled remaining three tubes one third full of copper sulfate solution.

4. Clean the metal strips by rubbing with sandpaper. Using a separate tube for each strip of metal, place strips of lead, zinc, and copper in each of the three kinds of solutions.

📛 **5.** After several minutes, examine the strips for evidence of a reaction; remove them from the solutions if necessary. Record your observations in the Data Table. Also note if the solution changed color.

Observations

DATA TABLE

	Lead Acetate	Zinc Sulfate	Copper Sulfate
Lead			
Zinc			
Copper			

1. Which metal did not react with any of the solutions it was placed in?

_____

2. Which metal reacted with all but its own solution?

_____

Analysis and Conclusions

1. List the metals in order of decreasing activity. _____

_____

2. How could you tell which of the three metals was the most active?

_____

_____

Critical Thinking and Application

1. Magnesium is more active than zinc. How would a strip of magnesium have reacted in the

three solutions you studied? _____

_____

2. Tin is less active than zinc but more active than lead. How would a strip of tin have

reacted in this investigation? _____

_____

3. A strip of silver does not react with any of the solutions tested. What must be true about

silver? _____

_____

4. What experiment could you perform in order to determine if iron is more active than

copper? _____

_____

_____

5. Metals like platinum and gold are often said to be inactive. What does this mean?

_____

_____

Going Further

1. Read about plating with copper or silver. How is plating done commercially? How could
   you do it in the laboratory?

2. Determine the activity of aluminum relative to the other metals.

_____ *Laboratory Investigation* _____

The Law of Definite Composition

Background Information

Many compounds are made of exactly the same elements but have very different physical and chemical properties. For example, carbon dioxide (CO_2), and carbon monoxide (CO), are both gases consisting of carbon and oxygen. Yet carbon dioxide is a harmless gas found in the body whereas carbon monoxide is a deadly gas when inhaled in sufficient amounts.

The reason for the difference between these two carbon–oxygen compounds is explained by the law of definite composition. This law states that the masses of the elements in a compound always occur in the same proportion. In other words, a carbon monoxide molecule consists of only 1 carbon atom and 1 oxygen atom. A carbon dioxide molecule consists of 1 carbon atom and 2 oxygen atoms. The difference in the number of oxygen atoms makes these two compounds very different from each other.

In this investigation you will compare the physical and chemical properties of water and hydrogen peroxide, both of which consist of hydrogen and oxygen.

Problem

How can two compounds consist of the same elements yet have different properties?

Materials *(per group)*

graduated cylinder
hydrogen peroxide, 3%
manganese dioxide
safety goggles
2 test tubes
test-tube rack
matches
2 wood splints

Procedure

1. Put on your safety goggles. Label one test tube H_2O (water) and the other H_2O_2 (hydrogen peroxide). Measure 5 mL of each compound and pour it into the appropriate test tube.

2. Observe the physical properties of each compound and record your observations in the Data Table on page 84.

3. Put a small amount of manganese dioxide on the tip of one of the wood splints and add a little to each test tube. If you see evidence of a chemical reaction occurring, perform the following step: Light the unused wood splint with a match. Blow out the flame so that the wood is glowing at the edges. Insert the glowing splint into the test tube(s) in which a chemical reaction is occurring. Record your observations in the Data Table.

Observations

DATA TABLE

Compound	Physical Properties	Reaction With Manganese Dioxide
Water (H_2O)		
Hydrogen peroxide (H_2O_2)		

Analysis and Conclusions

1. How do the physical properties of water and hydrogen peroxide compare?

_____

_____

_____

2. What effect did the manganese dioxide have on each compound?

_____

_____

_____

3. How do the chemical properties of water and hydrogen peroxide compare?

_____

_____

_____

4. How do the formulas for the two compounds differ? _____

_____

5. State a hypothesis to explain why water and hydrogen peroxide have different chemical

properties. _____

_____

Critical Thinking and Application

1. The atomic mass number of hydrogen is 1.0. The atomic mass number of oxygen is 16.0.

   a. What is the proportion by mass of hydrogen to oxygen in water?

   _____

   b. What is the proportion by mass of hydrogen to oxygen in hydrogen peroxide?

   _____

2. Explain how the law of definite proportions explains the fact that although water and hydrogen peroxide consist of the same elements, they have different properties.

   _____

   _____

   _____

   _____

3. Look up the atomic mass number of carbon in your periodic table. Mass number of

   carbon: _____

   a. What is the proportion by mass of carbon to oxygen in carbon monoxide?

   _____

   b. What is the proportion by mass of carbon to oxygen in carbon dioxide?

   _____

4. Explain how the law of definite proportions explains the fact that although carbon monoxide and carbon dioxide consist of the same elements, they have different properties.

   _____

   _____

Going Further

   The manganese dioxide used in this investigation is a catalyst. Using reference sources, find out what catalysts are and how they are used in chemical reactions. Describe an investigation you might perform to demonstrate the effect of a catalyst on a chemical reaction. Use a laboratory report format that includes title, problem, materials, procedure, observations, and conclusions.

_____ *Laboratory Investigation* _____

Comparing Covalent and Ionic Compounds

Background Information

Compounds are either covalent or ionic depending on the nature of the forces that hold them together. In ionic compounds, the force of attraction is between oppositely charged ions. This attraction is called an ionic bond. In covalent compounds, atoms are held together by an interaction between adjacent nuclei and shared electrons. These different forces account for many of the properties of ionic and covalent compounds, such as the degree of volatility (ability to turn into a gas) and solubility.

In this investigation you will examine the properties of a representative ionic compound, sodium chloride, and a representative covalent compound, paradichlorobenzene (PDB). The properties studied will be volatility, ease of melting, and solubility in water.

Problem

How do the properties of ionic and covalent compounds differ?

Materials *(per group)*

sodium chloride	Bunsen burner	ring stand with ring
paradichlorobenzene	wire gauze	safety goggles
evaporating dish	2 test tubes	fume hood (if available)

Procedure

1. Carefully smell each compound. If you can detect an odor, assume that the compound has a high volatility. Record your observations in the Data Table.

2. In turn, place small equal amounts of each substance in an evaporating dish. See Figure 1. If possible, perform the next step in a fume hood. If a fume hood is unavailable, keep the flame well away from the contents of the evaporating dish and make sure the room is well ventilated. Heat each sample with a burner flame and observe the time required to melt each sample. As soon as the PDB melts, remove the flame. Record your results in the Data Table.

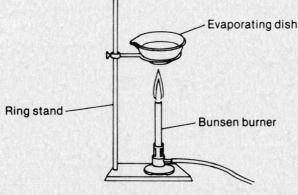

Figure 1

👁 **3.** Put a few small crystals of each substance in separate test tubes containing several milliliters of water at room temperature. Shake or stir and record in the Data Table how rapidly the substances dissolve in water.

Observations

DATA TABLE

Substance	Volatility	Melting Time	Solubility
Sodium chloride			
PDB			

1. Which compound was more volatile? _____

2. Which compound melted more quickly? _____

3. Which compound dissolved more easily in water?

_____

Analysis and Conclusions

1. Explain why the type of bond could determine the volatility of a substance.

_____

_____

_____

2. Does the strength of the bond have anything to do with the time it takes to melt a

substance? Explain. _____

_____

3. Water molecules have parts that are negatively charged and parts that are positively charged. Which substances tend to dissolve easier in water, ionic or covalent? Why?

_____

_____

_____

_____

Critical Thinking and Application

1. What do your data tell you about the melting points of ionic and covalent compounds? How can you tell? _____

_____

_____

2. Which do you think would be more dangerous near an open flame: an ionic or a covalent compound? Why? _____

_____

3. Which type of compound—ionic or covalent—would you expect to have a higher boiling point? Why? _____

_____

4. Suppose you had a sample of two compounds mixed together. Both compounds consist of fine white crystals. You know that one of the compounds is ionic and the other is covalent. How might you separate the two compounds?

_____

_____

_____

_____

Going Further

1. With adult supervision, test a variety of household materials to determine whether they are probably ionic or covalent. Vegetable oil, sugar, paraffin, and epsom salts are possible choices.

2. Certain substances when dissolved in water will conduct an electric current. Find out whether such substances are more likely to be ionic or covalent.

Laboratory Investigation

18

Chemical Synthesis

Background Information

The word synthesis means to put together. In a chemical reaction involving synthesis, two or more substances combine to produce a single, more complex substance. The combined substances can be elements, compounds, or both. A written chemical equation involving synthesis should follow this general pattern:

Element or compound + Element or compound → Compound

For example, when a metal combines with oxygen from the air, the synthesis reaction that occurs is called oxidation. A compound called a metal oxide is produced. The reaction follows the general pattern:

Metal + Oxygen → Metal oxide

In this investigation you will synthesize copper oxide by heating copper metal in air.

Problem

How can a synthesis reaction be recognized?

Materials (per group)

ring stand and ring
wire gauze
Bunsen burner
triple-beam balance
evaporating dish
copper powder
scoop
safety goggles
tongs

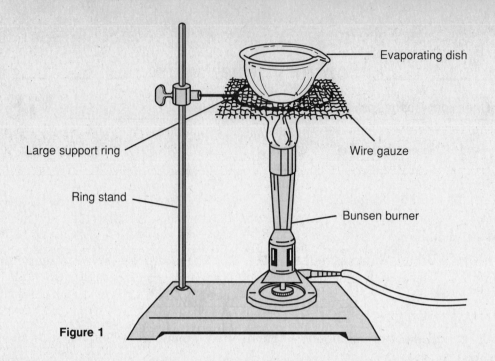

Evaporating dish

Large support ring

Wire gauze

Ring stand

Bunsen burner

Figure 1

Procedure

1. Set up the ring stand, ring, wire gauze, and Bunsen burner as shown in Figure 1.

2. Place the evaporating dish on the balance and find its mass to the nearest 0.1 g. Record the mass in Observations.

3. Add 5 g to the mass of the evaporating dish and move the riders on the balance to this number.

4. Using the scoop, slowly add copper powder to the evaporating dish until the pointer of the balance is on zero.

5. Place the evaporating dish containing the copper powder on the wire gauze. Make sure the copper powder is in a thin layer in the bottom of the dish.

6. Light the Bunsen burner and heat the evaporating dish for 5 to 10 minutes.

7. Turn off the Bunsen burner and allow the evaporating dish to cool for 5 to 10 minutes. Using the tongs, place the evaporating dish on the balance and find its mass. Record the mass in Observations.

Observations

1. Mass of empty evaporating dish _____

2. Mass of evaporating dish + copper powder _____

3. Mass of copper powder _____

4. Mass of evaporating dish + copper oxide after heating _____

_____

5. Mass of copper oxide _____

Analysis and Conclusions

1. What did you observe as a result of heating the copper powder that might indicate that a

   chemical reaction took place? _____

2. What kind of chemical reaction occurred? _____

3. What was the change in mass when the copper powder reacted with oxygen to form

   copper oxide? _____

   Was this change an increase or decrease in mass? _____

4. Was this reaction endothermic or exothermic? _____

   Explain. _____

   _____

5. Write a chemical equation for the synthesis reaction that took place.

   _____

Critical Thinking and Application

1. Explain why there was a change in mass as a result of heating the copper powder in the

   evaporating dish. _____

   _____

2. Find the percentage change in mass by using the following formula.

$$\text{Percentage change in mass} = \frac{\text{Change in mass}}{\text{Mass of copper}} \times 100 \text{ percent}$$

   _____

3. There are actually two different oxides of copper produced as a result of this reaction.
   They are copper(I) oxide and copper(II) oxide. If copper is changed to copper(I) oxide,
   the percentage change in mass is 12 percent. If copper is changed to copper(II) oxide,
   the percentage change in mass is 25 percent. What must have been produced as a result
   of your investigation to give the percentage change in mass you calculated?

   _____

   _____

4. Compare the percentage change in mass that you calculated with that calculated by your classmates. What variables would account for differences between your results and those

of your classmates? _____

_____

5. How could these variables be controlled so that the results obtained are more alike?

_____

_____

_____

6. Copper(II) oxide is black and copper(I) oxide is red. Using the scoop, examine the product of the reaction in the dish. Observe its color or colors. Does your observation

support your answer to question 3? Explain. _____

_____

_____

Going Further

Use references to find out about other synthesis reactions. If time permits, do these reactions under your teacher's supervision.

_____ *Laboratory Investigation* _____

Chemical Decomposition

Background Information

Chemical decomposition is the opposite of chemical synthesis. In a decomposition reaction, a single compound is broken down into two or more simpler substances. These substances can be elements, other compounds, or both. A written chemical equation involving decomposition should follow this general pattern:

Compound → Element or compound + Element or compound

For example, the compound potassium chlorate can be decomposed into potassium chloride and oxygen gas as a result of heating. Similarly, sodium chloride, or common table salt, can be decomposed into the elements sodium and chlorine by passing an electric current through it. This process is known as electrolysis.

In this investigation you will decompose water by electrolysis and determine the identity and relative amounts of the elements that are produced.

Problem

What are the products of the decomposition of water by electrolysis?

Materials *(per group)*

beaker, 600 mL or larger
bell wire
dry cell, 6 volt
graduated cylinder
2 ring stands with test-tube
   clamps
matches
safety goggles
2 M sulfuric acid
wire strippers
2 wood splints

Procedure

1. Put about 400 mL of water into the beaker. Fill each test tube with water. Holding your hand over the mouth of one test tube at a time to prevent spilling, turn each test tube upside down in the beaker. Clamp each test tube so that it is suspended just above the bottom of the beaker. See Figure 1.

2. Strip about 3 cm of insulation from one end of each piece of bell wire. Strip about 1 cm of insulation from the other end of each piece of bell wire. Attach the 1-cm bare end of one piece of wire to one of the terminals of the dry cell. **CAUTION:** *Do not attach the other wire to the other terminal yet.*

3. Bend the wires so that they trail over the edge of the beaker. Each 3-cm bare wire end should be placed in one of the test tubes. See Figure 1. Have your teacher check your setup to be sure it is correct before proceeding. After doing the next step, you will not be able to put your hand in the water.

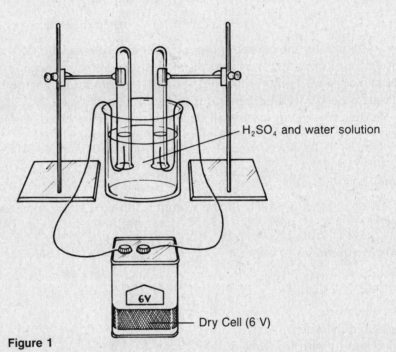

H_2SO_4 and water solution

6V

Dry Cell (6 V)

Figure 1

4. Attach the remaining loose end of wire to the other terminal of the dry cell. Put on safety goggles. Without splashing, carefully add 50 mL of 2-M sulfuric acid to the water in the beaker. Record your observations. **CAUTION:** *Do not put your hands in the beaker for any reason.*

5. Allow the reaction to proceed for about 10 minutes or until no water is left in one of the test tubes. Disconnect the wires from the dry cell.

6. Remove the test tube with the least amount of water in it from the clamp. Hold it with a paper towel and keep your thumb over the top. Have a member of your lab group light one of the splints so that it is flaming and put it in the test tube. Record your observations. **CAUTION:** *Be careful when working with a burning splint.*

7. Remove the remaining test tube from the clamp and follow the same procedure as in step 6, but this time blow out the flame before placing the splint in the test tube. Record your observations.

8. Dispose of your acid solution as instructed by your teacher.

Observations

1. What did you observe happening in the test tubes when you added the acid?

   _____

   _____

2. What did you observe when you put the flaming splint in the first test tube?

   _____

3. What did you observe when you put the glowing splint in the second test tube?

   _____

4. To which battery terminal (positive or negative) was the test tube with the greater

   amount of water connected? _____

5. To which battery terminal (positive or negative) was the test tube with the lesser amount

   of water connected? _____

Analysis and Conclusions

1. What happened when acid was added to each test tube?

   _____

   _____

2. What caused the water level in the test tubes to change?

   _____

   _____

3. What gas was produced in the test tube that had the lesser amount of water?

   _____

4. What gas was produced in the test tube that had the greater amount of water?

   _____

5. Is this reaction endothermic or exothermic? _____

   Explain. _____

   _____

6. Write a chemical equation for the decomposition reaction that took place.

_____

Critical Thinking and Application

1. Identify the gas that was produced at the positive terminal.

_____

2. Identify the gas that was produced at the negative terminal.

_____

3. Would you observe different results if you repeated the investigation but reversed the

terminals to which the wires were attached? _____

Explain. _____

_____

4. Why were different amounts of the two gases produced? *Hint:* Look at the chemical

formula for water. _____

_____

_____

5. Did the sulfuric acid undergo a chemical change? _____

Why was the sulfuric acid necessary? _____

_____

Going Further

The nitrogen cycle and the carbon–oxygen cycle occur in nature and consist of many synthesis and decomposition reactions involving these elements. Use references to find out about the steps in these cycles. Identify each step as either a synthesis or decomposition reaction.

_____ *Laboratory Investigation* _____

20 __

Single-Replacement Reactions

Background Information

In nature, elements can occur either free, meaning uncombined with other elements, or chemically combined in a compound. The tendency of a particular element to combine with other substances is a measure of the activity of that element. The more active an element is, the more likely it is to combine. In a single-replacement reaction, an uncombined element replaces a less active element that is combined in a chemical compound. The less active element is then freed from the compound.

For example, in the reaction

Zinc + Copper sulfate → Zinc sulfate + Copper

zinc replaces the less active copper, combines with sulfate, and frees the copper from the compound.

In this investigation you will observe how various metals undergo single-replacement reactions when placed in acid. If the metal is more active than the hydrogen in the acid, it will replace the hydrogen and hydrogen gas will be released.

Problem

How does a single replacement reaction occur?

Materials *(per group)*

safety goggles
5 test tubes
test-tube rack
1 M hydrochloric acid
graduated cylinder
zinc
copper
aluminum
iron
magnesium

Procedure

1. Label each test tube with the name of one of the metals listed in the materials.

⚠ 2. Put on your safety goggles. Carefully pour 5 mL of hydrochloric acid into each test
   tube.

👁 3. One at a time, place the appropriate metal in each test tube. Observe what happens to
   the metal in each test tube and feel each test tube as the reaction proceeds. Record your
   data in Observations.

4. When you have completed the investigation, carefully pour off the acid, rinse the metal
   several times with water, and put it into a container provided by your teacher. Do not put
   any unused metal in the sink.

Observations

1. Magnesium _____

_____

2. Aluminum _____

_____

3. Iron _____

_____

4. Copper _____

_____

5. Zinc _____

_____

Analysis and Conclusions

1. Write the single-replacement reaction that occurred between the acid and each metal.

   a. Magnesium _____

   _____

   b. Aluminum _____

   _____

   c. Iron _____

   _____

Name _____ Class _____ Date _____

    d. Copper _____

    _____

    e. Zinc _____

    _____

2. Were these reactions endothermic or exothermic? _____

Explain. _____

_____

Critical Thinking and Application

1. Which of the metals are more active than hydrogen? _____

_____

2. Which of the metals are less active than hydrogen? _____

_____

3. What could you do to prove that hydrogen gas was produced as a result of these

reactions? _____

_____

_____

4. The rate at which hydrogen gas is produced as a result of these single-replacement reactions is an indication of the relative activity of the metals. List the metals in order of

their activity from most active to least active _____

_____

5. Nonmetals can also be involved in single-replacement reactions. If chlorine is more active than bromine, write the equation for the reaction between chlorine and potassium

bromide. _____

_____

© Prentice-Hall, Inc.

101

Going Further

Identify each of the following chemical equations as representing a synthesis, decomposition, or single-replacement reaction. Write a balanced equation for each reaction.

1. Silver nitrate + Copper → Copper nitrate + Silver

_____

2. Hydrogen + Oxygen → Water

_____

3. Aluminum + Zinc chloride → Aluminum chloride + Zinc

_____

4. Aluminum hydroxide → Aluminum oxide + Water

_____

5. Barium chloride → Barium + Chlorine gas

_____

Laboratory Investigation

21

Double-Replacement Reactions

Background Information

Some of the most impressive chemical reactions are double-replacement reactions, also called ion-exchange reactions. In a double-replacement reaction, a clear solution of an ionic compound is added to a clear solution of another ionic compound. The positive ions of one compound react with the negative ions of the other compound to form a precipitate, a gas, or water. When a precipitate forms, the result can be very dramatic. The precipitate is an insoluble solid substance that may produce a sudden bright color in the remaining clear solution.

In this investigation you will perform a double-replacement reaction and observe and interpret the results.

Problem

How does a double-replacement reaction occur?

Materials (per group)

safety goggles
triple-beam balance
2 250-mL beakers
weighing paper
lead nitrate
potassium iodide
stirring rod
graduated cylinder

Procedure

👁 1. Put on safety goggles. Place a piece of weighing paper on the balance and note its mass.
⚗   Add 3 g to the mass of the paper and move the riders to this number. Measure out 3 g of lead nitrate and place it in one of the beakers. Discard the paper.

⚗ 2. Add 50 mL of distilled water to the beaker and stir thoroughly to make sure that all the solid has dissolved. Rinse off the stirring rod and wipe it dry. Label the beaker Lead nitrate solution.

3. Repeat steps 1 and 2 using potassium iodide. Label the beaker Potassium iodide solution.

4. Pour the solution from one beaker into the other beaker and observe the results. Stir with the stirring rod and observe.

5. To dispose of your product, put it in the waste container indicated by your teacher. Do not spill the product down the sink. Rinse the beaker once with tap water and dispose of this material in the waste container. Thoroughly wash the beakers and stirring rod with soap and water.

Observations

1. What did you observe when you mixed the lead nitrate with water?

_____

_____

2. What did you observe when you mixed the potassium iodide with water?

_____

_____

3. What did you observe when you mixed the two solutions together?

_____

_____

4. Did stirring the combination of the two solutions result in any change? _____

Explain. _____

_____

Analysis and Conclusions

1. What ions were present in the lead nitrate solution? _____

_____

2. What ions were present in the potassium iodide solution? _____

_____

3. Write an equation for the reaction that took place. _____

_____

Critical Thinking and Application

1. A double-replacement reaction is also called an ion-exchange reaction. Describe the exchange of ions that occurred in this investigation. _____

_____

_____

_____

2. What must always be one of the products of a double-replacement reaction?

_____

3. What must the other product(s) always be? _____

_____

4. Describe what would happen if the product you obtained in this reaction were filtered through a filtering apparatus. _____

_____

_____

Going Further

Identify each of the following chemical equations as representing a synthesis, decomposition, single-replacement, or double-replacement reaction. Write a balanced equation for each reaction.

1. Carbon monoxide → Carbon + Oxygen

_____

2. Sodium + Water → Sodium hydroxide + Hydrogen gas

_____

3. Aluminum sulfate + Barium chloride → Aluminum chloride + Barium sulfate

_____

4. Aluminum + Chlorine → Aluminum chloride

_____

5. Sodium carbonate + Calcium hydroxide → Sodium hydroxide + Calcium carbonate

_____

_____ *Laboratory Investigation* _____

Chapter 8   Chemical Reactions _____ **22** ___

Comparing Reaction Rate and Catalysts

Background Information

Catalysts are substances that speed up chemical reactions even though they themselves are not used up. A small amount of a catalyst may have a great effect upon a reaction. Catalysts are often used in industry to speed up production. In this investigation you will study a chemical reaction and determine which materials act as a catalyst to speed up the reaction.

Problem

How do catalysts speed up a chemical reaction?

Materials *(per group)*

7 test tubes
35 mL 3% hydrogen
   peroxide solution
small quantities:
   manganese dioxide
   chromium oxide
   calcium oxide
   aluminum oxide
   cobalt oxide
   silicon dioxide

Procedure

1. Pour about 5 mL of hydrogen peroxide into each of seven test tubes. Note if any gas is produced. Look for bubbles.

2. Add one of the other substances to each of six test tubes, using the seventh as a control. Note if any gas is produced. (The gas is oxygen.)

3. Record your observations in the Data Table.

Observations

DATA TABLE

Substance Added	Effect (Gas Produced?)
Manganese dioxide	
Chromium oxide	
Calcium oxide	
Aluminum oxide	
Cobalt oxide	
Silicon dioxide	
(Control)	

1. Which substances produced a gas (oxygen)? _____

_____

_____

2. Was there a difference in the rate at which the gas was produced? _____

Explain. _____

_____

_____

Analysis and Conclusions

1. Which substances acted as catalysts? _____

_____

2. Are some of the substances more effective catalysts than others?

_____

_____

3. How much manganese dioxide would be needed to catalyze a great amount of hydrogen

peroxide? Explain. _____

_____

Critical Thinking and Application

1. What is the purpose of the control in this investigation?

_____

_____

_____

_____

2. Based on this investigation, do you think that often more than one substance can act as a
catalyst in the reaction? Why? _____

_____

_____

_____

_____

3. Do you think that some substances might be better catalysts than others? Explain.

_____

_____

_____

_____

4. Can you think of circumstances in which the addition of a catalyst might not be a good
idea? _____

_____

_____

_____

_____

Going Further

1. Enzymes are catalysts produced in the body that help the body digest certain foods. Make
a list of several important enzymes and their function.

2. Newer cars are designed with catalytic converters that take the exhaust and change it into
harmless products before releasing the exhaust into the environment. Find out what
substances are changed and what they become.

_____ *Laboratory Investigation* _____

Testing Unknown Substances Using Acid–Base Indicators

Background Information

Indicators are special chemicals that can show whether a given substance is an acid, a base, or neither. Indicators usually react with an acid or a base to form a slightly different chemical with a different color. Some examples of indicators are litmus paper and phenolphthalein. In this investigation you will test two unknown substances to see whether they are acidic or basic.

Problem

How can you determine whether a substance is an acid or a base? What happens when an acidic solution and a basic solution are mixed together?

Materials *(per group)*

solution A
solution B
10-mL graduated cylinder
4 test tubes
stirring rod
red litmus paper
blue litmus paper
1 mL 1% phenolphthalein
   solution
wire gauze
ring stand and ring
Bunsen burner
magnifying lens
small pieces of zinc, 1 g
2 medicine droppers
safety goggles
heat-resistant gloves

Procedure

👁 **1. CAUTION:** *Put on safety goggles.*

👁 **2.** Obtain 5 mL of solution A in a test tube and 5 mL of solution B in another test tube. **CAUTION:** *Use care when measuring and pouring solutions A and B. Wash any spills immediately with cold water.* Label the test tubes appropriately A and B.

3. Using a medicine dropper, place a drop from test tube A on a piece of blue litmus paper. Record any color change of the litmus paper in the Data Table.

4. Using the same medicine dropper, place another drop from test tube A on red litmus paper. Record any color change in the Data Table.

5. Repeat steps 3 and 4 using solution B and a clean medicine dropper.

6. Put two drops of phenolphthalein solution into each test tube. Note the results in the Data Table.

7. Pour the contents of tubes A and B into a 200-mL beaker. Note the result of mixing the two solutions. Then place the beaker and its contents on a wire gauze on a ring stand as shown in Figure 1. Position a Bunsen burner beneath the beaker and light it. **CAUTION:** *Be careful when lighting and using the Bunsen burner.* Heat the beaker for 10 minutes or until the liquid has boiled away, leaving a dry residue.

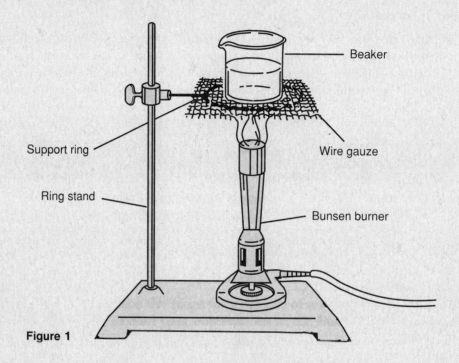

Figure 1

8. Allow the beaker to cool. Then examine the remaining residue with a magnifying lens.

9. Obtain 5 mL of the two solutions again in separate labeled test tubes. Put a few small pieces of zinc into each test tube and note the results in the Data Table.

Observations

DATA TABLE

Solution	Response to Litmus		Response to Phenolphthalein	Reaction With Zinc
	Red	Blue		
Solution A				
Solution B				

112

1. Which solution turned litmus paper red? _____

2. Which solution turned litmus paper blue? _____

3. Which solution produced a color change in phenolphthalein? _____

4. Which solution reacted with zinc to produce gas bubbles? _____

Analysis and Conclusions

1. Litmus paper turns blue in the presence of a base and red in the presence of an acid.

   Which solution, A or B, is an acid? _____ On a pH scale of 1 to 14, what would be the

   approximate pH of the solution you selected? _____

2. Phenolphthalein indicator turns bright magenta (purplish red) in solutions that have a pH greater than 8. Solution B was hydrochloric acid (HCl). Solution A was sodium hydroxide (NaOH). What do you think was the pH of the solution that resulted when you mixed equal amounts of solution A and solution B?

   _____

   What was the identity of the white residue remaining after the boiling?

   _____

3. What do you think was the identity of the gas given off when zinc reacted in one of the

   solutions? _____

   _____

4. Write the balanced equation for mixing solutions A and B together.

   _____

5. Write the balanced equation for the reaction that occurred between zinc and

   solution B. _____

Critical Thinking and Application

1. Based on the equation you wrote for mixing solutions A and B together, what is the general reaction for the combination of an acid and a base?

   _____

2. Based on the equation you wrote for the reaction between zinc and solution B, what happens when an acid comes in contact with a metal?

_____

3. Suppose you had mixed unequal amounts of solution A and solution B. What do you think the pH of the resulting solution would be?

_____

_____

4. Design an experiment in which you could investigate the effect of mixing unequal amounts of acid and base.

_____

_____

_____

Going Further

The indicator litmus is a commonly used lab compound. Find out where it was first obtained.

_____ *Laboratory Investigation* _____

Testing Commercial Antacids

Background Information

Common indigestion is often caused by excess stomach acid. Popular stomach remedies, or antacids, claim to remove the symptoms of acid indigestion by neutralizing excess stomach acid.

In this investigation you will test the effectiveness of several commercial antacids by determining whether the antacid will neutralize a given volume of hydrochloric acid.

Problem

Do commercial stomach remedies neutralize acid?

Materials *(per group)*

100-mL beaker
medicine dropper
HCl, 1 M
methyl orange indicator
several different commercial
    antacids
mortar and pestle
stirring rod
distilled water

Procedure

1. Pour 10 mL of HCl into a beaker.

 2. Put two to three drops of methyl orange indicator into the beaker and record the color in the Data Table.

 3. Fill a clean dropper with the liquid antacid and add the liquid drop by drop to the beaker, stirring after each drop. In the Data Table, record the number of drops you add and any color changes you see.

4. Continue to add drops and stir until there is no more color change.

5. Use the mortar and pestle to grind one of the antacid tablets into a fine powder. While grinding, slowly add 10 mL of distilled water.

6. Fill a clean dropper with the powder-water mixture. Fill a clean beaker with 10 mL of HCl. Repeat steps 2, 3, and 4 for this mixture. (If you run out of tablet mixture, you may have to grind another tablet.)

7. Repeat steps 5 and 6 for the second brand of antacid tablet.

Observations

DATA TABLE

Color of Indicator in Acid	Substance Added to Acid	Number of Drops	Change in Color	Other Observations

Analysis and Conclusions

1. Can you conclude that commercial antacids do neutralize stomach acid? _____

   On what do you base this conclusion? _____

   _____

2. What must be the nature of the substances that make up antacids? How can you tell?

   _____

   _____

   _____

Critical Thinking and Application

1. Is it possible to determine from this investigation whether one type of antacid is more

   effective, or better, than another? Explain. _____

   _____

   _____

   _____

2. When testing some of the antacids, you may have observed a gas being released. What

   was this gas? _____

3. What is the general chemical reaction for the process that produced the gas you named

   in question 2? _____

   _____

Going Further

Collect advertisements for various types of antacids from magazines and newspapers. Have a class discussion or debate about whether the claims of such ads are "scientific."

_____ *Laboratory Investigation* _____

Acids and Bases From Home

Background Information

The science laboratory is not the only place where acids and bases are found. Many items commonly found at home are acids or bases. For example, many of the foods you eat contain acids. Commonly used cleaning products owe their effectiveness to the fact that they are alkaline, or contain bases.

In this investigation the strength of common acidic and basic substances found in the home will be determined using a method known as titration. To titrate an acidic substance, a basic solution whose concentration is known is added to the acid until the acid is neutralized. A color change in an acid–base indicator is used to determine when neutralization has occurred. The amount of basic solution added to achieve neutralization indicates the comparative strength of the acid. A basic solution is titrated in exactly the same way, except that an acid solution of known concentration is added.

Problem

How can the acidity or alkalinity of common household substances be determined?

Materials *(per group)*

3 different fruit juices
milk
4 liquid cleaning products
antacid tablets, cut into quarters
white vinegar (5%)
safety goggles
stirring rod
4 test tubes
test-tube rack
medicine dropper
dropper bottle of
   phenolphthalein
graduated cylinder
test-tube brush

Procedure
Part A

1. Pour 5 mL of each fruit juice into its own test tube. Pour 5 mL of milk into a fourth test tube. Record the color of each liquid in Data Table 1.

2. Put four drops of phenolphthalein indicator into each test tube. Note the color of each juice and of the milk. Record your observations in Data Table 1.

3. Add the quartered antacid tablets one at a time to one of the fruit juices, stirring after each quartered tablet is added. When a color change occurs, stop adding tablets to that test tube. Record your observations in Data Table 1.

4. Repeat the procedure for the remaining test tubes, making sure you wash off the stirring rod before proceeding to the next sample.

5. Wash the test tubes and stirring rod in preparation for performing Part B of the investigation.

Part B

1. Pour 5 mL of each liquid cleaning product into its own test tube. Record the color of each liquid in Data Table 2.

2. Put four drops of phenolphthalein indicator into each test tube. Note the color of each cleaning product. Record your observations in Data Table 2.

3. Add the vinegar one drop at a time to one of the cleaners, stirring after each drop is added. When a color change occurs, stop adding vinegar to that test tube. Record your observations in Data Table 2.

4. Repeat the procedure for the remaining test tubes, making sure you wash off the stirring rod before proceeding to the next sample.

5. Wash the test tubes and stirring rod thoroughly.

Observations

DATA TABLE 1

Liquid	Color	Color With Phenolphthalein	Number of Antacid Quarters Needed for Neutralization	Color After Neutralization
Juice				
Juice				
Juice				
Milk				

DATA TABLE 2

Cleaner	Color	Color With Phenolphthalein	Number of Vinegar Drops Needed for Neutralization	Color After Neutralization

Analysis and Conclusions

1. In what pH range (acid or basic) were the juices before neutralization?

_____

In what pH range was the milk? _____

2. Which of the beverages is probably the strongest acid? _____

Explain your conclusion. _____

_____

_____

3. Which of your beverages is probably the weakest acid? _____

Explain your conclusion. _____

_____

_____

4. List the four beverages in order of acidity from strongest to weakest.

_____

_____

5. In what pH range (acid or basic) were the cleaners before neutralization?

_____

6. Which of your cleaners is probably the strongest base? _____

Explain your conclusion. _____

_____

_____

7. Which of your cleaners is probably the weakest base? _____

Explain your conclusion. _____

_____

_____

8. List the four cleaners in order of alkalinity from strongest to weakest. _____

_____

Critical Thinking and Application

1. You may have found that the results you obtained were different from those of other groups. What variables might have affected your results in this investigation?

_____

_____

_____

2. What could you use to check the accuracy of your results in this investigation? Describe

your procedure. _____

_____

_____

3. How could you determine the acidity or alkalinity of other substances found in your home? Write an investigation that you might do using pH paper as an indicator. Include the problem, hypothesis, materials, procedure, observations, and conclusions.

_____

_____

_____

_____

_____

_____

_____

_____

_____

Going Further

Obtain pH paper from your teacher and with his or her approval, perform the investigation you described above.

_____ *Laboratory Investigation* _____

Fractional Distillation

Background Information

Fractional distillation is a process by which different liquids combined in a mixture can be separated on the basis of their different boiling points. During the process, the mixture is heated slowly so that each substance, or fraction, in the mixture reaches its boiling point and vaporizes. As it vaporizes, it leaves the liquid and passes to an area where it is cooled and condensed back to its liquid phase. The fraction is now separated from other substances in the mixture. Fractional distillation is used in the petroleum industry to separate crude oil into its many useful parts, which include gasoline, jet fuel, lubricants, and waxes.

In this investigation you will perform a fractional distillation of a mixture of water, isopropyl ("rubbing") alcohol, and ethylene glycol.

Problem

How can a mixture of liquids be separated by fractional distillation?

Materials *(per group)*

3 large test tubes
ring stand
test-tube clamp
test-tube rack
2-hole rubber stopper (to fit test
    tube)
400-mL beaker with crushed ice
several boiling chips
right-angle glass tubing
rubber tubing, 40 cm
Bunsen burner
Celsius thermometer
isopropyl alcohol
ethylene glycol
graph paper

Procedure

🔺 1. Half-fill a test tube with the liquid mixture provided by your teacher. Put the test tube in the test-tube rack while you set up the apparatus.

🔺 2. Set up the apparatus as shown in Figure 1. Note that the bulb of the thermometer is near the top of the test tube, not in the liquid. Place a few boiling chips in the test tube.

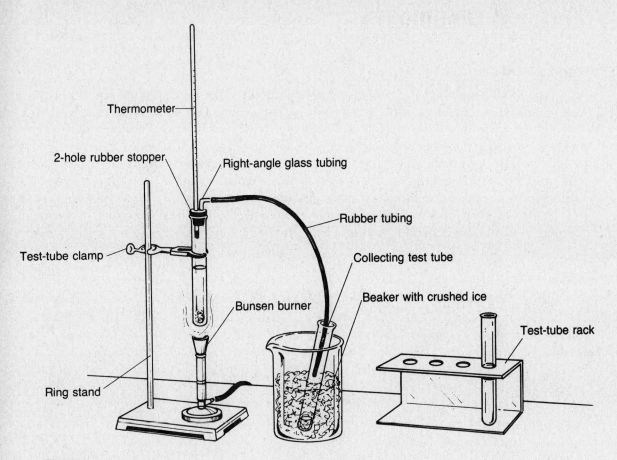

Figure 1

🔥 3. Light the Bunsen burner and slowly heat the test tube. Make sure that the flame is a moderate one. Do not allow the liquid to boil rapidly. Record the temperature at 1-minute intervals in the Data Table.

4. When the temperature stops rising, you should notice a liquid beginning to collect in the test tube in the beaker of crushed ice. Note this temperature in the Data Table. **CAUTION:** *Do not allow the rubber tubing to touch the liquid being collected.*

5. When the temperature begins rising again, remove the collecting test tube from the crushed ice and replace it with an empty test tube. Place the test tube with the collected liquid in the test-tube rack.

6. When the temperature again stops rising, you should notice a liquid beginning to collect in the test tube. Note this temperature in the Data Table. Do not allow the rubber tubing to touch the liquid being collected.

🖐 7. When the temperature begins rising again, turn off the Bunsen burner and allow the heated test tube to cool before taking apart the apparatus.

Observations

DATA TABLE

Time (min)	1	2	3	4	5	6	7	8	9	10	11	12	13	14	15
Temperature (°C)															

1. At what temperature did the first liquid fraction begin to collect in the cool test tube?

_____

2. At what temperature did the second liquid fraction begin to collect in the cool test

tube? _____

3. Describe the liquid remaining in the heated test tube.

_____

4. Carefully smell the separated fractions and describe their odor.

_____

_____

Analysis and Conclusions

1. Draw a graph of your data. Plot time along the horizontal axis and temperature along the vertical axis.

2. On the basis of your observations of boiling temperature, odor, and appearance, identify

the three fractions. _____

_____

3. Explain how each liquid was separated and then collected.

_____

_____

_____

_____

_____

_____

Critical Thinking and Application

1. Did the complete separation of liquid fractions take place? _____

   Explain. _____

   _____

   _____

   _____

2. Under what circumstances would it be more difficult to separate the fractions in a liquid

   mixture? _____

   _____

   _____

   _____

3. How do you know that fractional distillation is a physical separation, not a chemical

   one? _____

   _____

   _____

   _____

Going Further

Solid substances can also be separated into useful components by a similar process called destructive distillation. Do library research to find out how destructive distillation is accomplished and what kinds of products result.

Laboratory Investigation

27

Tensile Strength of Natural and Synthetic Polymers

Background Information

Tensile strength of a material is the amount of force required to break a wire or thread of that material. Tensile strength is a measure of the overall strength of the molecular forces that hold the substance together. Synthetic polymers such as polyester and nylon were developed to be stronger than natural polymers. In this investigation you will test the tensile strength of threads made of cotton (a natural polymer) and polyester, and you will draw conclusions as to which is stronger.

Problem

What are the tensile strengths of cotton, polyester, and cotton-covered polyester?

Materials (per group)

spring balance, 20-N capacity
polyester, cotton, and cotton-
   covered polyester threads of
   equal diameter
ring stand and ring
liquid bleach
3 beakers
cardboard
scissors
glass-marking pencil
safety goggles

Procedure

1. Obtain three beakers. Label the first beaker Polyester, the second beaker Cotton, and the third beaker Cotton-Covered Polyester.

2. Place three 40-cm-long pieces of polyester thread in the appropriate beaker. Repeat for the cotton and cotton-covered polyester threads.

3. Pour enough liquid bleach into each beaker to cover the bottom and the threads.

4. Set the beakers aside for 30 minutes.

5. Cut a piece of cardboard 1 cm × 5 cm. Fold the cardboard in half so that you have a V-shaped wedge that is 2.5 cm long.

6. Insert the legs of the cardboard wedge into the slot of the spring balance. See Figure 1.

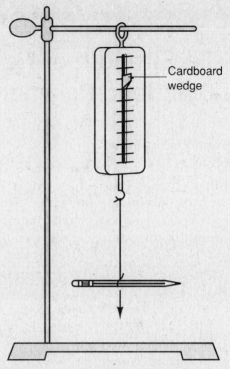
Cardboard wedge

7. Hang the top loop of the spring balance on the crossbar of the ring stand as shown in Figure 1.

8. Cut three 40-cm pieces of polyester threads. Tie loops on both ends for each of the three pieces.

9. Slip the loop of one end of one of the pieces of thread over the bottom hook of the spring balance. Slip a pencil or pen through the bottom loop.

10. Set the cardboard wedge to zero. Pull down very, very slowly on the pencil until the thread breaks.

Figure 1

11. Read the value on the scale that is opposite the top of the cardboard wedge. Record the tensile force to the nearest 0.1 N in the Data Table.

12. Obtain three trials for the polyester threads by repeating steps 9 through 11 two more times.

13. Repeat steps 8 through 12 for the cotton and then the cotton-covered polyester threads. Record all data.

14. After 30 minutes have elapsed, pour off the liquid bleach and rinse the beakers and threads several times with water. Dry the threads by pressing them between paper towels.

15. Now test these threads in the same way as before. Record your data in the Data Table.

Observations

DATA TABLE

Trial	Without Bleach			With Bleach		
	1	2	3	1	2	3
Polyester						
Cotton						
Cotton-covered polyester						

1. In the space below, calculate the average tensile force for the three trials for each material both without bleach and with bleach.

2. How did the average values without bleach compare with the average values with bleach?

_____

_____

Analysis and Conclusions

1. Which material has the greatest tensile strength?

_____

2. Which material loses the most tensile strength when soaked in bleach?

_____

Critical Thinking and Application

1. What general statement can you make about the effect of bleach on fibers?

_____

_____

2. Parachutes, once made of the natural fiber silk, are today made of the synthetic polymer Dacron. What possible reason can you offer for this change?

_____

_____

_____

_____

3. Which do you think would last longer, a shirt made of cotton or a shirt made of

   polyester? Explain your answer. _____

_____

_____

_____

4. The label in a 100-percent cotton dress reads, "Do not bleach." Why do you think this

   label is included? _____

_____

_____

_____

_____

5. The most common thread used in materials is cotton-covered polyester. Is this thread used because of its high tensile strength? What other reasons could justify its widespread

   use? _____

_____

_____

_____

Going Further

Test the tensile strength of nylon and wool. Using nylon and wool materials, repeat steps 8 through 15 of Procedure.

_____ Laboratory Investigation _____

Chapter 11   Radioactive Elements _____ **28** _____

Half-Life of a Capacitor

Background Information

Radioactive material decays by emitting alpha or beta particles. During the process of decay, an atom of the original element decays into a different element. The time it takes for one half of all the atoms to decay into another element is called the half-life of the substance. Half-lives of elements can vary from microseconds to billions of years.

In this investigation you will determine the half-life of an electric capacitor. A capacitor stores a large quantity of electric charge and then slowly releases that charge. The same concept of radioactive half-life can be applied to a discharging capacitor. Unlike radioactive materials, capacitors do not give off radiation.

Problem

How do you determine the half-life of a discharging capacitor?

Materials *(per group)*

capacitor, 2000 to 6000
     microfarads
DC voltmeter
pegboard
DC power source
knife switch
connecting wires
clock with second hand

Procedure

1. Connect the capacitor, voltmeter, power source, and knife switch as shown in Figure 1.
   Note: *Make sure the positive terminal of the capacitor is connected to the positive terminal of the power source.*

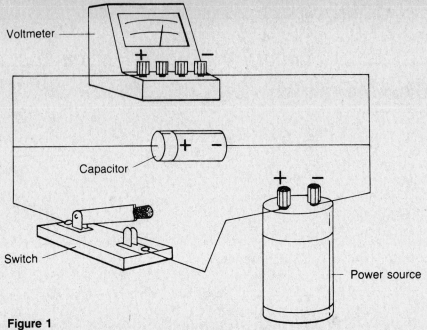

Figure 1

2. Study the scale on the voltmeter carefully. Because you will have to read the voltage very quickly, notice what each division on the voltmeter scale represents.

3. One student in each group will be the timer. This student will watch the clock and will alert the others in the group to each 10-second interval. A second student will watch and read the voltmeter and call out its voltage at each 10-second interval. A third student will record the voltage in the proper 10-second interval in the Data Table.

4. **CAUTION:** *Be very careful when using electricity. Before your group closes the switch, have your teacher check your setup.* Close the switch and read the voltage. Do not start timing yet. Record this voltage in the Data Table next to 0 seconds.

DATA TABLE

Time (sec)	Voltage (V)	Time (sec)	Voltage (V)	Time (sec)	Voltage (V)
0		80		160	
10		90		170	
20		100		180	
30		110		190	
40		120		200	
50		130		210	
60		140		220	
70		150		230	

5. Start timing the 10-second intervals the instant the switch is opened. During this time, the timer should call out "ten seconds," while the voltage reader tells what the voltage is. **Note:** *The student who reads the voltage should try to anticipate each 10-second interval. Otherwise, it may take more than 10 seconds to decide what the reading is.*

6. Continue taking readings until you are unable to read the amount of remaining voltage.

Observations

1. In Figure 2, draw a graph of your results. Place the time, in seconds, on the horizontal axis and the voltage on the vertical axis.

GRAPH

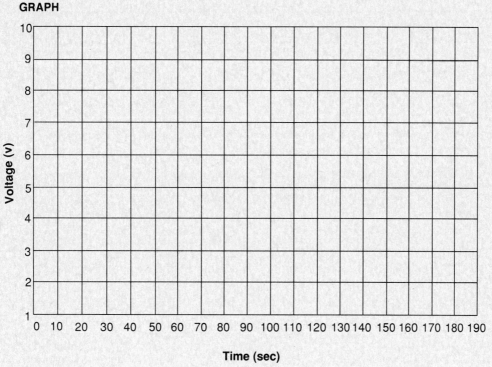

Figure 2

Analysis and Conclusions

1. Using the graph in Figure 2, find the half-life of the capacitor. To do so, find one half of the highest voltage on the vertical axis. For example, if the highest voltage is 10, one half of it is 5. Then move horizontally across from this point until you intersect your curve. Now vertically move down until you meet the horizontal axis. This is the time it takes for one half of the voltage to decay. What is this number?

_____

2. How long did it take to reach one fourth of the original voltage?

_____

Critical Thinking and Application

1. If the original sample of a radioactive element were increased, what would happen to its

   half-life? Explain. _____

   _____

   _____

2. After a period of four half-lives of a radioactive element has passed, what fraction of its

   original mass still remains? _____

3. If an element gives off an alpha particle (helium nucleus) during radioactive decay, what
   happens to its atomic mass? Its atomic number? What happens to the atomic mass and
   atomic number of an element that gives off a beta particle (electron) during radioactive

   decay? _____

   _____

   _____

4. Why are elements with long half-lives used to date fossils of ancient plants and animals?

   _____

   _____

   _____

   _____

   _____

   _____

Going Further

The half-life of the capacitor can be decreased by adding a resistor of at least 1000 ohms
in parallel with the voltmeter. Determine the half-life of the capacitor when the resistor is
added.

_____ *Laboratory Investigation* _____

29

Analyzing Motion

Background Information

Without complex and expensive instruments, it is difficult to obtain an accurate analysis of the motion of an object. However, by graphing the distance vs. time of an object, it is possible to determine at a glance whether an object is accelerating, decelerating, or moving at a constant speed during a particular period of time.

A recording or acceleration timer is a simple device used to obtain quantitative information about the motion of an object. During the operation of the timer, a moving object pulls a piece of paper through the timer and under a hammer that strikes the paper and records a series of dots. The more slowly the object moves, the closer together the dots. The faster the object moves, the farther apart the dots. The distance between dots measures the distance covered by the moving object in between two strikes of the hammer on the paper. The time period between the strikes, which will be called a "tik," measures the time it takes to go that distance.

In this investigation you will use a recording timer to obtain information about a moving object. You will then record that information on a graph and analyze and interpret the results.

Problem

How can a graph be used to analyze the motion of an object?

Materials *(per group)*

recording (acceleration) timer
   with tape
Hall's carriage, skateboard, or
   roller skate
30-cm ruler
graph paper
masking tape
meterstick

Procedure

1. Set up the recording timer on the floor as demonstrated by your teacher.

2. Cut a length of recording tape 2 m long. Insert one end under the hammer of the timer and tape that end to the object you are using: cart, skateboard, or roller skate. The remaining tape should trail out behind in a straight line. See Figure 1.

3. While one lab partner starts the timer, another should give the skate a strong push across the floor away from the timer. Make sure that the skate pulls the tape completely through the timer. A third lab partner should be positioned to catch the moving object.

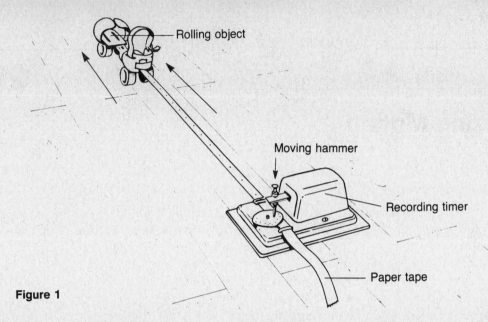

Figure 1

4. Remove the tape from the object and mark the end that was attached to the skate "START." Move ahead 1 or 2 cm from here and mark this dot zero. Number every *second* dot after this 1, 2, 3, and so on. The numbers represent the time, measured in tiks, taken to travel the distance between the dots. This will give you the time information you need for your graph.

5. Using your 30-cm ruler, measure the distance to the nearest tenth of a centimeter between every set of numbers you placed on your tape. Record this information in the Data Table. This will give you the information about the distance your object traveled that you need for your graph.

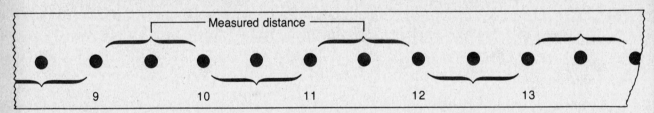

Figure 2

6. Draw a graph of the information you recorded in the Data Table. Plot time in tiks on the X axis and distance traveled in cm on the Y axis.

7. Using a colored pencil, draw a "curve of best fit" over your graph.

Observations

DATA TABLE

Interval 0 - 1 - 2 - 3 - 4 - 5 - 6 - 7 - 8 - 9 -10 -11 -12 -13 -14 -15 -16 -17 -18 -19 -20 -21 -22 -23 -24 - 25

Tik	1	2	3	4	5	6	7	8	9	10	11	12	13	14	15	16	17	18	19	20	21	22	23	24	25
Distance (cm)																									

Analysis and Conclusions

1. What were the units of time used in this investigation? _____

   Why could seconds or minutes not be used? _____

   _____

   _____

   _____

2. How did the dots on the tape measure the speed at which the object moved?

   _____

   _____

   _____

   _____

3. Did your graph show that your object moved in a smooth, regular motion?

   _____

   Explain. _____

   _____

   _____

   _____

4. Why was it necessary to draw a "curve of best fit?"

   _____

   _____

   _____

   _____

5. Examine your "curve of best fit." Was your object accelerating, decelerating, or traveling

   at constant speed? _____

   _____

   _____

   _____

Critical Thinking and Application

1. Calculate the average velocity in cm/tik of the object. Find the difference between the fastest velocity and the slowest velocity and divide the result by 2.

   _____

2. Does the average velocity that you calculated tell how fast the object was really going at

   any instant of time? _____

   Explain your answer. _____

   _____

   _____

3. What are some variables that might have prevented your graph from being smooth like

   the "curve of best fit"? _____

   _____

   _____

Going Further

Use the recording timer to investigate the motion of falling objects. Place the timer at the top of a high shelf or cabinet and drop a mass attached to the recording tape to the floor. Record your data and draw a graph. Compare your results with the motion of the rolling object.

_____ *Laboratory Investigation* _____

30

Calculating Acceleration

Background Information

Acceleration is the rate of change of velocity. Suppose a car accelerates from rest to

10 m/sec in 5 sec. Its acceleration is: $\dfrac{10 \text{ m/sec} - 0 \text{ m/sec}}{5 \text{ sec}} = 2$ m/sec/sec. In this

investigation you will determine the acceleration of a moving object.

Problem

How is the acceleration of a moving object calculated?

Materials (*per group*)

bicycle
2 stopwatches
masking tape
meterstick

Procedure

1. Find a level surface suitable for riding a bicycle.

2. Place a piece of masking tape on the ground at the starting point.

3. Using a meterstick, measure 20 m from the first tape. Mark the 20-m distance with another piece of masking tape.

4. Place a third piece of tape 5 m past the 20-m tape. Your tapes should look like Figure 1.

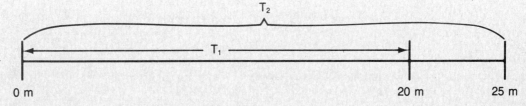

Figure 1

5. The bicycle will start at the zero meter mark.

6. Have one person stand with stopwatch 1 at the 20-m mark. Have another member of your group stand with stopwatch 2 at the 25-m mark.

7. One person will act as the starter. When the starter says "go," begin riding the bicycle. At the same time, have your classmates start both stopwatches.

8. Stopwatch 1 will record the time (T_1) it takes for the bicycle to reach the 20-m mark. Stopwatch 2 will time the full 25 m (T_2).

9. Try several practice runs.

10. When you obtain consistent time results, take three time trials and record the times in the Data Table.

Observations

DATA TABLE

Trial	T_1 (sec)	T_2 (sec)
1		
2		
3		

1. Calculate the time it took the bicycle to move from the 20-m mark to the 25-m mark for each trial (T_v). $T_v = T_2 - T_1$.

2. Calculate the velocity (v_1) between the 20-m mark and 25-m mark for each trial.

   $$\text{Velocity} = \frac{5m}{T_v}$$

3. The velocity calculated in question 2 was an average velocity. Since the bicycle was accelerating, the velocity was continually changing from the 20-m mark to the 25-m mark. We will assume that the average velocity you calculated is the same as the instantaneous velocity halfway between the two marks. The total time (T_t), therefore, should be T_1 plus one-half of T_v. Calculate T_t for each trial.
   $T_t = T_1 + \frac{1}{2}T_v$.

Analysis and Conclusions

1. Calculate the acceleration of the bicycle for each trial. Acceleration $= \dfrac{V_1 - V_0}{T_t}$
   Remember: Since the bicycle started from rest, V_0 is 0 m/sec.

2. Based on this investigation, what measurements must be made in order to calculate the acceleration of an object that begins at rest?

   _____

   _____

   _____

Critical Thinking and Application

1. What hidden variable in this investigation might make it difficult to obtain consistent

   results in the three trials? _____

   _____

   _____

   _____

2. Can acceleration ever be negative? Explain your answer.

   _____

   _____

   _____

   _____

3. Suppose you wanted to determine the acceleration of a ball rolled along a flat surface. What factor might make this calculation more difficult than determining the acceleration

   of a bicycle? _____

   _____

   _____

   _____

4. Suppose the acceleration of a bicycle were calculated as zero. Assuming the bicycle is not at rest, what must be true about its motion?

_____

_____

_____

Going Further

What is the acceleration of an object that takes 7 sec to change its velocity from 25 m/sec to 39 m/sec?

_____ *Laboratory Investigation* _____

31 ____

Construction and Use of an Accelerometer

Background Information

A device called an accelerometer is often used for measuring acceleration. Acceleration is a change in the rate of velocity of an object. Since velocity involves both speed and direction, acceleration measurements can be of speed or direction. In this investigation you will construct an accelerometer and use it to determine the direction of acceleration.

Problem

How is the direction of acceleration determined by an accelerometer?

Materials *(per group)*

1-l jar with lid
string
lead sinker or large machine nut
candle
matches

Procedure

1. Tie the lead sinker to a piece of string.

2. Cut the string so that it is slightly shorter than the length of the jar.

3. Attach the free end of the string to the center of the bottom of the lid using melted candle wax.

4. Allow the candle wax to completely harden. Test to see if the wax holds the string and sinker. If it does not, add more candle wax to the point of attachment.

5. Completely fill the jar with water.

6. Place the sinker in the water and tightly screw on the lid. Your accelerometer should look like the one in Figure 1.

Figure 1

7. Hold the jar steady and start walking. Record the position of the sinker as you accelerate and as you walk at a constant speed.

8. Record the position of the sinker as you stop.

9. Walk around in a circle about 1 m in diameter. Record the sinker positions.

Observations

1. What is the direction of the sinker as you accelerate from rest?

_____

_____

2. What is the direction of the sinker when you are walking at a constant speed in a straight line?

_____

_____

3. What is the position of the sinker when you are walking at a constant speed in a circle?

_____

_____

Analysis and Conclusions

1. When you accelerate, does the sinker move backward or does the bottle move forward?

_____

2. Does the sinker point toward or away from the direction of acceleration?

_____

_____

3. Based on your observations, how does the rate at which your speed changes affect the position of the sinker?

_____

_____

Critical Thinking and Application

1. What would happen if you accelerated the bottle downward? Upward?

_____

_____

_____

_____

2. How do the movements of the sinker relate to your movements when you are traveling in a bus?

_____

_____

_____

_____

3. There is a circular ride in most amusement parks called a spinner. The people who ride on it stand up around the walls while it spins rapidly. As the ride continues, the floor drops out, but the people remain where they are. Analyze the motion of the people in relation to your observations of the motion of the sinker.

_____

_____

_____

_____

Going Further

Hold your accelerometer while sitting in a car. Observe the position of the sinker as the car accelerates, moves at a constant speed, stops, and turns corners.

Laboratory Investigation

32

Investigating Friction

Background Information

One of the forces you have studied is friction. Friction is a retarding force. This means it lessens the effect of other forces. Friction, therefore, causes a "loss" of useful energy in many mechanical devices. This energy, of course, is not really lost but is transferred to heat energy at the point of contact.

In this investigation you will explain why the movement of one object over another produces heat and how changes in design can reduce friction. You will also learn how surface area, texture, and weight influence friction.

Problem

What are some factors that affect friction?

Materials *(per group)*

spring balance
rectangular block of wood fitted
   with a metal eye
large piece of sandpaper

Procedure

1. Suspend a block of wood from the spring balance and obtain its weight in newtons. Record the weight below.

Weight of block _____

2. Place the block on the lab table with its larger surface (side A) downward. See Figure 1.

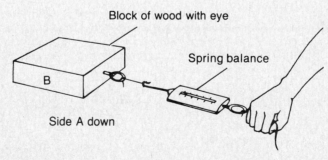

Block of wood with eye

Spring balance

B

Side A down

Figure 1

3. Keep the spring scale level with the table and pull the block along the table. In Data Table 1 record the force indicated on the spring scale needed to start the block moving. Also record the force indicated on the spring scale once the block is sliding evenly along the lab table.

4. Repeat step 3 twice, recording your readings in Data Table 1. Calculate the average for the starting friction and the sliding friction.

5. Calculate the surface area for side A (area = length × width), and record it in the space provided.

6. Place the block on the lab table with its smaller surface (side B) downward. See Figure 2.

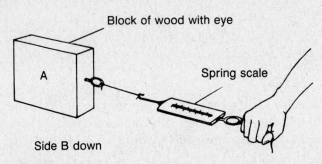

Figure 2

7. Repeat steps 3 and 4. Record your readings in Data Table 1.

8. Calculate the area for side B and record it in the space provided.

9. Repeat steps 1 through 8, sliding the surfaces of the block over a piece of sandpaper. Record your readings in Data Table 2 for side A and for side B.

10. Obtain a block of wood from a classmate, along with the data on its weight. Place it on top of your block so that the original A side is facing down. Record the weight of the two blocks and the sliding force required to move them across the lab table.

Weight of two blocks _____ Average sliding force _____

If time permits, borrow a third block and repeat.

Weight of three blocks _____ Average sliding force _____

Observations

DATA TABLE 1

Surface Area of Side A _____ cm²

Trial	Starting Friction (N)	Sliding Friction (N)
1		
2		
3		
Average		

Surface Area of Side B _____ cm²

Trial	Starting Friction (N)	Sliding Friction (N)
1		
2		
3		
Average		

DATA TABLE 2

Side A

Trial	Starting Friction (N)	Sliding Friction (N)
1		
2		
3		
Average		

Side B

Trial	Starting Friction (N)	Sliding Friction (N)
1		
2		
3		
Average		

How did the starting friction compare to the sliding friction?

_____

Analysis and Conclusions

1. What do you think accounts for the difference between the starting friction and the sliding friction?

_____

_____

2. Based on your data, how does the surface area influence the sliding force of friction?

_____

_____

_____

3. Based on your data, how does texture influence the sliding force of friction?

_____

_____

_____

4. How does weight influence the sliding force of friction?

_____

_____

_____

Critical Thinking and Application

1. List two situations in which friction can be helpful.

   _____

   _____

2. List two ways you could reduce the friction between two or more surfaces.

   _____

   _____

3. Why do wheels reduce the force of friction? _____

   _____

4. Which task would require more effort, pushing a 1-kg box across an ordinary floor or pushing a 2000-kg box across a frictionless floor? Explain your answer.

   _____

   _____

   _____

   _____

Going Further

1. Determine the advantages of lubricants such as grease and oil by performing a similar experiment.

2. Determine what happens to automobile motor oil when the engine heats up. Why is it important to have a heavier oil in summer than in winter?

Name _____ Class _____ Date _____

—— *Laboratory Investigation* ——

Chapter 13   The Nature of Forces   **33** __

Determining Acceleration Due to Gravity

Background Information

If air resistance is small, the rate at which a body falls is constant, regardless of its mass. The rate at which a body falls is determined by the gravitational force exerted on the body. On the surface of the Earth, acceleration due to gravity is close to 9.8 m/sec^2. In this investigation you will determine acceleration due to gravity using two different methods.

Problem

How can acceleration due to gravity near the surface of the Earth be determined?

Materials *(per group)*

string or wire about 1.5 m
    long
hooked weight, 500 g
timer
buret
pie plate
meterstick
beaker
ring stand with buret clamp

Procedure

Part A   Measuring Acceleration Due to Gravity Using a
        Pendulum

1. Place the ring stand on a table so that the clamp hangs over the side of the table. See Figure 1. Tie one end of the string to the clamp. Attach the 500-g weight to the other end of the string.

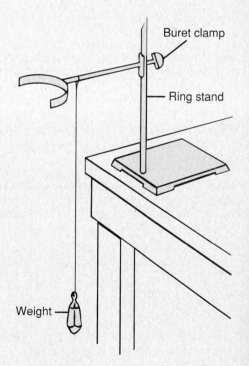

Buret clamp

Ring stand

Weight

Figure 1

149

2. Pull the weight back about ten degrees from its rest position. Release the weight and record in Data Table 1 the time (T) in seconds it takes to make 20 complete swings. One complete swing is back and forth.

DATA TABLE 1

Length (L) (m)	Time (T) 20 swings (sec)

3. Measure the length (L) of the wire or string from the center of the weight to the ring stand. Record this length to the nearest 0.01 m in the Data Table.

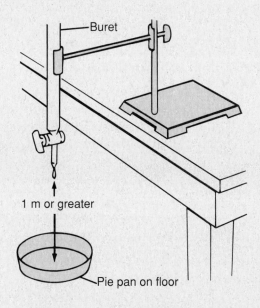

Part B Measuring the Acceleration of a Water Drop

1. Attach the buret to the ring stand with the buret clamp. See Figure 2. Fill the buret about three fourths full of water.

2. Place the pie pan on the floor beneath the buret. The pie pan should be at least 1 m below the base of the buret.

3. Adjust the drip rate so that one drop just leaves the buret when the previous drop hits the pie pan. Watch the drop at the buret and listen for the sound.

Figure 2

4. After adjusting the drip rate, record in Data Table 2 the number of seconds it takes for 100 drops to hit the pie plate. Keep the level of the water in the buret approximately constant by refilling it with a beaker.

DATA TABLE 2

Distance (d) (m)	Time (T) 100 drops (sec)

5. Measure the distance (d) from the tip of the buret to the pie plate. Record this distance to the nearest 0.01 m in the Data Table.

Observations
Part A

1. Calculate the time (T) for a single swing. (Divide the time for 20 swings by 20.)

2. Calculate the acceleration due to gravity in m/sec^2 using the formula:

$$A_G = \frac{39.5 \cdot L}{T^2}$$

where A_G = acceleration of gravity, L = length in meters, and T = time in seconds for one swing.

Part B

3. Calculate the time (T) for a single water drop to fall. (Divide the time for 100 drops by 100.)

4. Calculate the acceleration due to gravity using the formula:

$$A_G = \frac{2D}{T^2}$$

where A_G = acceleration of gravity, D = distance in meters, and T = time in seconds for one drop.

Analysis and Conclusions

1. The acceleration of gravity is approximately 9.8 m/sec^2. Which method was more

   accurate? _____

2. Can you offer possible reasons for your answer to question 1?

   _____

   _____

   _____

   _____

   _____

   _____

Critical Thinking and Application

1. Compare the motion of the object in Part A with the motion of the water droplets in Part B. How did the force of gravity influence each one?

_____

_____

_____

_____

_____

2. Study the formula used to calculate acceleration due to gravity in Part A. Assuming that A_G is constant, what must be true about the relationship between the length of the string and the time it takes for the pendulum to make one complete swing?

_____

_____

_____

3. Suppose you performed Part A using strings of varying lengths. How would you expect your calculated value of A_G to compare with the results you obtained in this investigation?

_____

_____

4. Study the formula you used to calculate acceleration due to gravity in Part B. How is the time taken for one droplet to fall related to the distance it falls?

_____

_____

Going Further

1. Perform Part A again, but this time attach a feather to the string instead of a weight.

   How does that affect your results? Why? _____

   _____

2. Perform Part B again, but this time use vegetable oil instead of water. How does that

   affect your results? _____

Laboratory Investigation

Chapter 13   The Nature of Forces

34

Weight and the Force of Gravity

Background Information

There is a difference between mass and weight. The mass of an object is defined as the amount of matter it contains. The weight of an object is determined by the force of gravity on its mass.

You have used a triple-beam balance to measure mass. To measure weight, a spring balance is used. Because weight is the downward force that results from the pull of gravity on an object, when a weight is attached to a spring the downward force will stretch the spring. The greater the weight of the object, the more the spring stretches.

If known masses are attached to a spring, the amount of stretch (weight) caused by different masses can be determined.

In this investigation you will measure how much a spring stretches as weight is applied to it. You will then determine the relationship between mass and weight.

Problem

How can a spring be used to measure the force known as weight?

Materials (*per group*)

ring stand	15 washers
large ring	2 large paper clips (washer
meterstick	hooks)
clamp	100-g mass
spring	

Procedure
Part A

1. Attach the ring to the ring stand and hang the spring from it.

2. Clamp the meterstick to the ring stand so that the 100-cm mark is resting on the table top and the spring is close to, but not touching, the meterstick. Attach the washer hook to the bottom of the spring. See Figure 1.

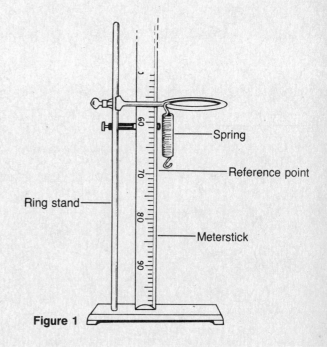

Figure 1

3. Note the number on the meterstick, to the nearest tenth of a centimeter, that is just even with the bottom of the spring. This number will be your reference point. Record this number in the Data Table.

4. Attach five washers to the washer hook and note the number on the meterstick that is just even with the bottom of the spring now. Record this number in the Data Table.

5. Repeat step 4 with 10 washers and then 15 washers added to the hook.

6. Remove the washers *five at a time* until no washers remain. Each time you remove five washers, note the number on the meterstick that is just even with the bottom of the spring. Record.

Part B

1. Note the reference point again. Record in Observations for Part B.

2. Hang a 100-g mass from the spring and note the number on the meterstick that is just even with the bottom of the spring. Record this number in Observations for Part B.

Observations
Part A

DATA TABLE

Number of Washers	Reading of Meterstick	Change in Length of Spring
0		
5		
10		
15		
10		
5		
0		

Part B

1. Reference point _____ cm

2. Meterstick reading with 100-g mass _____

3. Change in length of spring _____

Analysis and Conclusions

1. Draw a graph of your results in the Data Table. Label the vertical axis "Stretch (cm)" and the horizontal axis "Number of washers."

2. How much did the length of the spring change as each group of five washers was

added? _____

3. How much did the length of the spring change as each group of five washers was

removed? _____

4. How do your answers to questions 2 and 3 compare? _____

Explain. _____

_____

_____

_____

5. How does the shape of your graph illustrate your answers to questions 2 and 3?

_____

_____

_____

_____

Critical Thinking and Application

1. What force acts on the objects you attached to the spring? _____

2. In terms of forces, explain why the spring stretched as more washers were added.

_____

_____

_____

_____

3. In Part B you added a known mass to the spring. Since you know the amount by which
this known mass stretched the spring, calculate the mass of five washers.

_____

What is the mass of one washer? _____

4. Why do spring balances vary in accuracy? _____

_____

_____

_____

5. How is the maximum capacity of a spring balance determined?

_____

_____

_____

Going Further

Use the results obtained in Part B to calculate the masses of other objects. Verify your results by finding their mass on a balance. If your results differ, which do you think is more accurate, the balance or the spring? Explain.

_____ *Laboratory Investigation* _____

35 ____

Finding the Center of Gravity

Background Information

You should remember the difference between mass and weight. The mass of an object is defined as the amount of matter it contains. The weight of an object is determined by the force of gravity on the object. Because an object has mass, the Earth has an attraction for it. This force of attraction is called gravity. Gravitational force gives the object weight.

Regardless of the size and shape of an object, its weight seems to be concentrated at one point. This point is called the center of gravity. It is as if the force of attraction between the Earth and the object were acting at this one point alone.

In this investigation you will determine the center of gravity of an irregularly shaped object.

Problem

How can the center of gravity of an irregularly shaped, flat object be determined?

Materials (*per group*)

cardboard square (about 30 cm ×
    30 cm)
scissors
ruler
hole puncher
small metal weight or heavy
    washer
string (about 40 cm)
pencil
pegboard attached to wall
pegboard hook

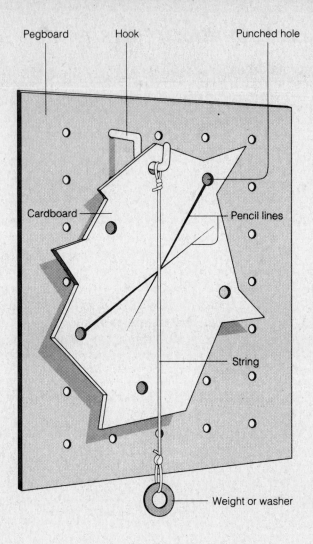

Pegboard   Hook   Punched hole

Cardboard —   Pencil lines

String

Figure 1   Weight or washer

Procedure

1. Cut the cardboard square into an irregular shape. Punch at least five holes around its edge.

2. Hang the cardboard from the pegboard hook by passing the hook through one of the punched holes. The diameter of the holes must be larger than that of the hook so that the cardboard hangs freely.

3. Attach the weight or washer to the string. Hang the string from the hook so that it hangs straight down and freely in front of the cardboard. Use the ruler and pencil to mark on the cardboard the straight line made by the string.

4. Repeat steps 2 and 3 until you have hung the cardboard from each of its holes.

Observations

Describe the appearance of the lines on the cardboard.

_____

_____

_____

In the space below draw a sketch of your cardboard after you have completed the Procedure.

Analysis and Conclusions

1. Where is the center of gravity of the cardboard? Why is this point the center of gravity?

   _____

   _____

   _____

   _____

2. Try to balance the cardboard on the end of your finger. At what point does the object

   balance? _____

   Why? _____

   _____

3. Could the method used in this investigation also be used to determine the center of

   gravity of a regularly shaped object? _____

Critical Thinking and Application

1. The center of gravity is sometimes called the center of mass. Explain why these terms are

   interchangeable. _____

   _____

   _____

   _____

2. A tightrope walker will fall if he leans too far over to one side. Relate this to the concept of the center of gravity. _____

_____

_____

_____

3. You can probably bend over and touch your toes without bending your knees. However, you could not do this exercise if your heels and back are against a wall. Try it. Explain this in terms of the center of gravity. _____

_____

_____

_____

Going Further

Repeat this activity using a ring-shaped piece of cardboard that has a large hole at the center. Does there actually need to be any matter at the center of mass of an object?

_____ *Laboratory Investigation* _____

36

Relating Archimedes' Principle of Buoyancy

Background Information

Fluids exert a pressure in all directions. The force that pushes upward in a fluid is called buoyancy. The upward buoyant force of a fluid opposes the downward force of gravity on an object placed in the fluid. According to Archimedes' principle, the buoyancy of an object equals the weight of the fluid the object displaces.

Weight and mass are not the same thing. It happens, however, that it is more convenient to test Archimedes' principle in the laboratory using measurements of mass rather than measurements of weight. The buoyancy of an object can be determined in terms of the mass of water the object displaces. This method works because mass and weight are proportional anywhere on the Earth.

If a solid piece of metal is placed in water, the metal will displace a volume of water equal to the metal's own volume. One milliliter of water has a mass of 1 g. So the volume of water displaced equals the mass of the water displaced. And the mass of water displaced equals the volume of the object. The buoyancy of the object in water, therefore, is the same value as the volume of the object.

An object placed in water appears to lose mass. This apparent loss in mass is equal to the mass of the displaced water, or the volume of the object. So a 100-g object that has a volume of 25 mL will have an apparent mass of 75 g (100 − 25) when placed in water.

In this investigation you will determine the mass of a metal object in air. Then you will suspend the object in water and determine the mass again. You will then compare the apparent loss in mass with the volume of the displaced water.

Problem

How does buoyancy relate to the apparent loss of mass of an object?

Materials *(per group)*

centigram balance
25-mL graduated cylinder
100-mL beaker
metal object
thread
ring stand with support ring
wire gauze

Procedure

1. Tie the metal object to the thread. Suspend the object in air by tying the thread to the hook above the balance pan of the centigram balance. Record the mass of the object to the nearest 0.1 g in the Data Table.

2. Set up the ring stand and support ring covered with wire gauze next to the balance so that a beaker may be placed under the metal object.

3. Half-fill the beaker with water. Set up the metal object, thread, and beaker of water as shown in Figure 1. Do not remove or touch the balance pan.

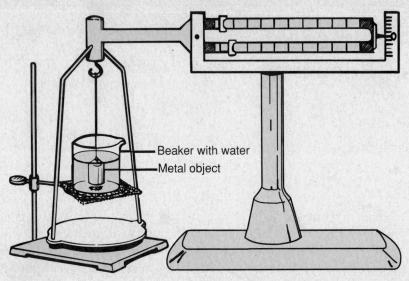

Beaker with water
Metal object

Figure 1

4. Make sure the metal object is completely submcrgcd in the water and is not touching the sides or bottom of the beaker.

5. Record the mass of the object in water to the nearest 0.1 g.

6. Place about 10 mL of water in the graduated cylinder. Record the volume to the nearest 0.1 mL.

7. Carefully place the metal object in the graduated cylinder. Record the new volume of the water to the nearest 0.1 mL.

Observations

DATA TABLE

Mass of object in air	____ g
Mass of object in water	____ g
Volume of water before adding object	____ mL
Volume of water after adding object	____ mL

1. Determine the loss of mass (buoyancy) of the object (mass in air − mass in water).

_____

2. Determine the volume of water displaced by the object.

_____

_____

3. Determine the mass of water displaced. Hint: 1 g of water = 1 mL of water.

_____

_____

Analysis and Conclusions

1. Is the buoyancy of the object about the same as the mass of water displaced?

_____

_____

2. Why is the loss of mass of the object only an apparent loss?

_____

_____

Critical Thinking and Application

1. A dancer finds that it is easier to lift a leg while standing in a swimming pool than while

standing on the floor. Why? _____

_____

_____

_____

2. People undergoing physical therapy after an injury often find it helpful to perform

exercises in water. Why? _____

_____

_____

_____

3. Explain why it is important in this investigation that the metal object not be touching the

bottom or sides of the beaker. _____

_____

_____

_____

4. Suppose two blocks of identical shape and size were placed in water. Block A is made of wood and block B is made of iron. How would the buoyant force on these two objects compare? Why? Assume both blocks sink below the water line.

_____

_____

_____

5. Explain what happens when a swimmer floats.

_____

_____

_____

Going Further

Put some water and ice in a glass, and mark the level of the top of the water on the side of the glass. When the ice melts, observe whether the level of the top of the water is higher, lower, or the same as before. Discuss your observation with your classmates and teacher.

_____ *Laboratory Investigation* _____

Can You Work More Efficiently?

Background Information

Work is applying a force to an object to move the object a certain distance in the direction of the force. If you pick up a book, you are doing work because you are exerting an upward force and moving an object in the same direction.

By using a simple machine, you can make work easier. For certain tasks, you can make work easier by decreasing the effort force required to move a resistance force. In other words, a smaller effort force can be applied to move a heavy mass. This is the concept of mechanical advantage.

In this investigation you will see how the mechanical advantage of a simple machine can be changed to enable you to work more efficiently.

Problem

Can the mechanical advantage of a simple machine be altered?

Materials *(per group)*

heavy string, 65 cm long
4 thin wooden rods: 1, 7 cm
   long; 2, 14 cm long;
   1, 20 cm long
book
2 tables or desks to serve as
   supports
watch or clock with second hand

Procedure

1. Place the two tables or desks close enough together so that the 14-cm wooden rod can rest on both.

2. Tie one end of the string securely to a book. Tie the other end securely to the wooden rod. See Figure 1.

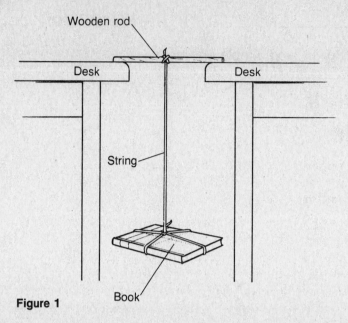

Wooden rod

Desk   Desk

String

Figure 1   Book

3. Rotate the wooden rod so that the string starts to wrap around it and the book begins to rise. Continue rotating the rod until you have raised the book as far as it can go. Determine how long it takes to do this. Record the time in the Data Table.

4. Lower the book to the floor. Tie the 7-cm rod to the other rod so that they are at right angles to each other. See Figure 2.

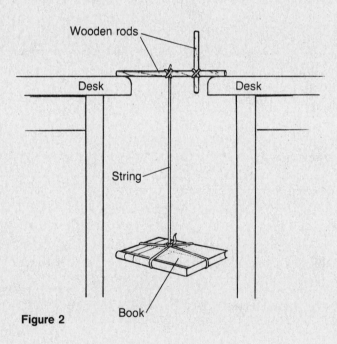

Wooden rods

Desk   Desk

String

Figure 2   Book

5. Use this shorter rod as a handle and rotate it to raise the book as before. Again determine how long it takes to do this and record the time in the Data Table.

6. Repeat steps 4 and 5 using the 14-cm rod and the 20-cm rod. Record your observations in the Data Table.

Observations

DATA TABLE

Book Raised by	Time (sec)	Relative Effort
Horizontal rod		
7-cm rod		
14-cm rod		
20-cm rod		

Analysis and Conclusions

1. Is there an advantage to using the handle to raise the book? Explain.

_____

_____

2. Which handle made the work easiest? _____

3. What simple machine is being used in this investigation? _____

   Explain the role of each of the two rods in this simple machine.

_____

_____

4. What is mechanical advantage? _____

_____

5. What part of this simple machine determines its mechanical advantage?

_____

Critical Thinking and Application

1. How did the use of a simple machine make you more efficient?

_____

_____

_____

2. Explain why with this simple machine work is made easier but does not increase.

_____

_____

_____

_____

3. What law is followed by your answer to question 2?

_____

4. What other simple machine could be used to raise the book?

_____

Going Further

Repeat this investigation using two books and four books. Determine the effect of increasing the resistance force on the mechanical advantage.

_____ *Laboratory Investigation* _____

The Inclined Plane

Background Information

Any slope along which an object (a resistance force) is moved from a lower level to a higher level is considered an inclined plane. Stairs, ramps, and roadways that go uphill are examples of inclined planes.

Because there is usually a large amount of friction between the inclined plane and the object being moved, two kinds of mechanical advantage (MA) need to be considered: ideal mechanical advantage and actual mechanical advantage. Ideal mechanical advantage does not take friction into account and is calculated by dividing the length of the plane (the effort distance) by the height of the plane (the resistance distance).

Actual mechanical advantage takes the effort needed to overcome friction into account. It is calculated by dividing the resistance force by the effort force. Because friction cannot be completely eliminated, the actual mechanical advantage is always less than the ideal mechanical advantage.

In this investigation you will see how an inclined plane is used as a simple machine and how friction affects its mechanical advantage.

Problem

How is an inclined plane used as a simple machine?

Materials *(per group)*

wood board about 1 m long
  × 15 cm wide
spring balance
resistance (object such as book
  or small wood block)
string
meterstick
ring stand
clamp

Procedure

1. Using the spring balance, find the weight of the object and record it in the Data Table.

2. Measure the length of the wood board and record it in the Data Table. This length will be the same for all parts of this investigation.

3. Raise one end of the board 8 cm above the level of the ring stand and clamp it to the ring stand.

4. Use the string to attach the spring scale to the object. Then use the spring scale to pull the object up the length of the board slowly and steadily. Note the force needed to do this and record it in the Data Table.

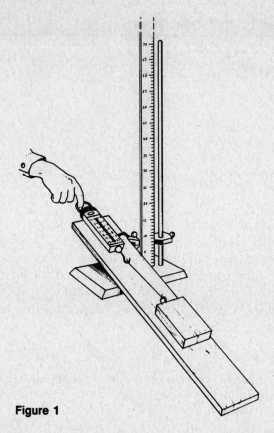

Figure 1

5. Raise the board 15, 30, and 40 cm above the level of the ring stand. Repeat step 4 for each height.

Observations

DATA TABLE

Height of Ramp	Length of Ramp	Resistance Force	Effort Force
8 cm	cm	N	N
15 cm	cm	N	N
30 cm	cm	N	N
40 cm	cm	N	N

Analysis and Conclusions

1. Calculate the actual mechanical advantage (AMA) of the inclined plane when its height is

a. 8 cm _____   c. 30 cm _____

b. 15 cm _____   d. 40 cm _____

2. Calculate the ideal mechanical advantage (IMA) of the inclined plane when its height is

a. 8 cm _____   c. 30 cm _____

b. 15 cm _____   d. 40 cm _____

3. How does the actual mechanical advantage compare with the ideal mechanical advantage for each height of the inclined plane?

_____

Critical Thinking and Application

1. How do you account for the fact that the actual mechanical advantage and the ideal

mechanical advantage are not the same? _____

_____

_____

_____

_____

2. What general statement can be made about the height of an inclined plane and its actual

and ideal mechanical advantage? _____

_____

_____

_____

_____

3. Explain your answer to question 2. _____

_____

_____

_____

_____

4. What happens to the energy that is used to overcome friction?

_____

_____

5. In a real machine, why is the work output always less than the work input?

_____

_____

Going Further

1. Design an investigation to test various ways to reduce friction in an inclined plane. With your teacher's permission, perform the investigation.

2. Cut a piece of paper in the shape of a right triangle with a long hypotenuse. With a pencil or pen, shade the hypotenuse at the edge of the paper. Wrap the triangle around a pencil, making sure that the shaded edge is facing out so that it is visible. What simple machine does this resemble? Explain why a screw is considered to be a modified inclined plane.

Laboratory Investigation

39

Simple Machines—Levers

Background Information

Simple machines make work easier to do. One way to express the benefit of using machines is called mechanical advantage (MA). The mechanical advantage of a machine is a number without units. If the mechanical advantage is more than 1, the machine makes work easier by multiplying the effort force. In other words, it causes an effort to seem larger than it actually is when acting against a resistance. If the mechanical advantage is less than 1, the machine makes work easier by allowing the resistance to move farther and faster than the effort. If the mechanical advantage is exactly 1, the machine makes work easier by changing the direction in which the effort must be applied.

A lever is a simple machine that involves two forces and a pivot point called a fulcrum. The force the user applies to the lever is called the effort or the effort force. The force against which the effort acts is called the resistance or the resistance force.

There are three classes of levers. The position of the two forces with respect to the fulcrum determines the class of the lever. In this investigation you will see how different positions of the effort, resistance, and fulcrum affect the mechanical advantage of the lever.

Problem

How does changing the positions of the effort, resistance, and fulcrum affect the mechanical advantage of a lever?

Materials *(per group)*

meterstick
spring balance
string
1-kg mass (or larger)
meterstick clamp or holder to
  serve as fulcrum

Procedure

1. Hang the mass from the spring balance to determine its force (weight) in newtons. Record this number in Observations as R.

2. Set up a first-class lever with the fulcrum at the 50-cm mark on the meterstick. Place the resistance (mass) and the effort (spring balance) at the distances indicated as resistance distance and effort distance, respectively, in A of Data Table 1. The effort force is the reading on the spring balance when the balance just balances the resistance. Calculate the mechanical advantage for this first-class lever. Record in Data Table 1.

3. Repeat step 2 three more times using the effort distances and resistance distances given for positions B, C, and D in Data Table 1.

4. Set up a second-class lever with the fulcrum 10 cm from the end of the meterstick. Place the resistance (mass) and the effort (spring scale) at the distances indicated in A of Data Table 2. Apply the effort and record the effort force reading on the spring scale. Calculate the mechanical advantage for this second-class lever. Record in Data Table 2.

5. Repeat step 4 two more times using the distances given for positions B and C in Data Table 2.

6. For the third-class lever, do not use the meterstick clamp as the fulcrum. Place the end of the meterstick on the tabletop. This will be your fulcrum. Place the resistance (mass) and the effort (spring scale) at the distances indicated in A of Data Table 3. Apply the effort and record the effort force reading on the spring scale. Calculate the mechanical advantage for this third-class lever. Record in Data Table 3.

7. Repeat step 6 two more times using the distances given for positions B and C in Data Table 3.

Observations

R = _____ N.

DATA TABLE 1 First-Class Lever: Fulcrum at 50 cm

Position	Effort Distance	Resistance Distance	Effort Force	Mechanical Advantage $\left(\frac{R}{E}\right)$
A	40 cm	40 cm		
B	40 cm	20 cm		
C	40 cm	10 cm		
D	20 cm	40 cm		

DATA TABLE 2 Second-Class Lever: Fulcrum at 10 cm from end of meterstick

Position	Effort Distance	Resistance Distance	Effort Force	Mechanical Advantage $\left(\frac{R}{E}\right)$
A	50 cm	40 cm		
B	50 cm	25 cm		
C	50 cm	10 cm		

DATA TABLE 3 Third-Class Lever

Position	Effort Distance	Resistance Distance	Effort Force	Mechanical Advantage $\left(\frac{R}{E}\right)$
A	20 cm	80 cm		
B	40 cm	80 cm		
C	60 cm	80 cm		

Analysis and Conclusions

1. In the first-class lever, how did the effort force compare with the resistance force when the effort distance was equal to the resistance distance?

   _____

2. What was the mechanical advantage of the first-class lever in which the effort distance

   was equal to the resistance distance? _____

   _____

3. In the second-class lever, how does the effort force compare with the resistance force?

   _____

4. In the second-class lever, was the mechanical advantage the lowest when the resistance

   was close to the fulcrum or close to the effort? _____

   _____

5. In the second-class lever, was the mechanical advantage the greatest when the resistance was close to the fulcrum or close to the effort?

   _____

   _____

6. Which third-class lever had the greatest mechanical advantage?

   _____

   _____

7. Which third-class lever had the least mechanical advantage?

   _____

   _____

Critical Thinking and Application

1. In a first-class lever, where would you place the effort and resistance forces to have the

   greatest possible mechanical advantage? _____

   _____

   _____

2. In a second-class lever, how did moving the fulcrum closer to the resistance affect the

amount of effort needed to balance the resistance? _____

_____

_____

How did it affect the mechanical advantage? _____

_____

_____

3. If you wanted to have the greatest possible mechanical advantage for a third-class lever,
would you move the effort closer to the fulcrum or closer to the resistance?

_____

Explain. _____

_____

4. If the mechanical advantage of a third-class lever is always less than one, what is its

benefit? _____

_____

_____

Going Further

   Make a list of at least 15 items in your home that are levers. Indicate the class of lever to
which each item belongs.

Laboratory Investigation

40

Pulleys As Simple Machines

Background Information

Pulleys are simple machines that are used in different ways to lift objects. The simplest kind of pulley is a grooved wheel around which a rope is pulled.

Pulleys can be used to change the direction of an applied force. For example, a pulley attached, or fixed, to the top of a flagpole allows you to raise the flag *up* by pulling *down*.

A combination of fixed and movable pulleys is called a pulley system, or block-and-tackle. A pulley system is used to multiply effort force in lifting heavy objects. Pulley systems are commonly seen around construction sites.

In this investigation you will see how different pulleys are used and determine the mechanical advantage of each.

Problem

How are pulleys used to raise objects? How is the mechanical advantage of a pulley or pulley system determined?

Materials *(per group)*

2 single pulleys	1 m nylon fishing line	spring balance
2 double tandem pulleys	ring stand and large ring	1-kg mass, or larger

Procedure

1. Find the resistance force of the mass you are using by attaching it directly to the spring balance. Record this resistance in the Data Table as the resistance for all of the pulley arrangements.

2. Set up a single fixed pulley as shown in Figure 1. Pull down on the spring balance to lift the mass. The reading on the balance shows the amount of effort needed to lift the resistance. Record this number in the Data Table.

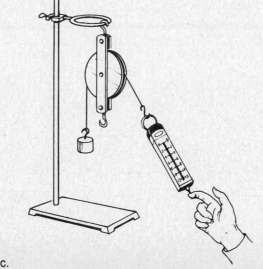

Figure 1

3. Set up a single movable pulley as shown in Figure 2. Lift the mass by pulling up on the spring scale. The reading on the balance shows the amount of effort needed to lift the resistance. Record this number in the Data Table.

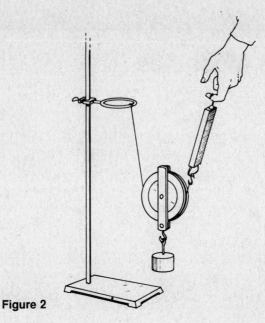

Figure 2

4. Set up the pulley system shown in Figures 3, 4, and 5. For each pulley system, measure the amount of force needed to lift the resistance and record it in the Data Table.

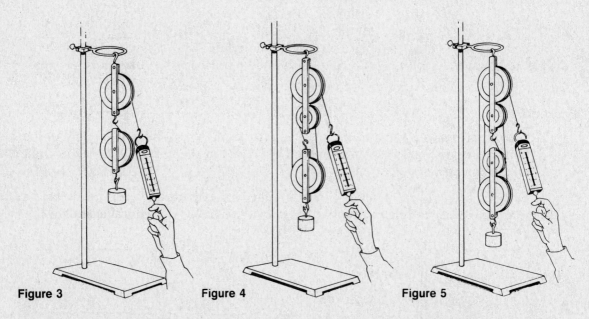

Figure 3   **Figure 4**   **Figure 5**

5. Calculate the mechanical advantage for each pulley and record these numbers in the Data Table.

Observations

DATA TABLE

Pulley Arrangements	Resistance (R)	Effort (E)	Mechanical Advantage (R ÷ E)
Single fixed			
Single movable			
Single fixed and single movable			
Double fixed and single movable			
Double fixed and double movable			

Analysis and Conclusions

1. Was there a difference in the mechanical advantages you calculated for the single fixed

pulley and the single movable pulley? _____ Explain your answer.

_____

_____

_____

2. As you added pulleys to the system, what happened to the amount of effort force needed

to raise the mass? _____

_____

_____

3. How does the type of pulley or pulley system affect the mechanical advantage?

_____

_____

_____

Critical Thinking and Application

1. If a simple machine has a mechanical advantage of 1, effort force is not multiplied.

Which type of pulley has a mechanical advantage of 1? _____

What is the practical use of this pulley? _____

_____

2. To determine the mechanical advantage of a pulley or pulley system without arithmetic calculations, it is possible to simply count the number of sections of rope that support the resistance mass. The end section, to which the balance is attached, counts as a supporting section of rope *only when pulled up*. Using Figures 1 through 5, determine the number of supporting rope sections for each type of pulley.

a. Figure 1 _____   d. Figure 4 _____

b. Figure 2 _____   e. Figure 5 _____

c. Figure 3 _____

3. Do the values obtained in question 2 agree with the calculated mechanical advantage in

the Data Table? _____ Explain your answer. _____

_____

_____

4. Using two double pulleys, draw an arrangement of the pulleys that would give you a mechanical advantage of 5.

5. When using any simple machine, you never "get something for nothing." Although the amount of effort force needed to lift a mass is reduced in a pulley system, something else is increased. What must be increased as the amount of effort force is decreased?

_____

_____

6. Explain your answer to question 5 in terms of work input and work output.

_____

_____

_____

_____

Going Further

Visit a construction site or an automobile repair shop that has a hoist to remove the engine from an automobile. Find out how pulley systems are used in these situations. Write a report of your findings.

_____ *Laboratory Investigation* _____

Investigating Factors Affecting a Pendulum

Background Information

A pendulum demonstrates many of the laws of physical science. Several related factors affect the behavior of the pendulum. These factors include the length of the arc, the length of the pendulum, the mass, and the number of swings per minute. In this investigation you will study the behavior of a pendulum as several factors are changed.

Problem

How do various factors affect the behavior of a pendulum?

Materials *(per group)*

2-m length of cord
1-kg mass
support
0.5-kg mass

Procedure

1. Tie a cord at least 2 m in length to a support from the ceiling or doorway so that it can swing freely. Attach the 1-kg mass securely at the end of the cord. See Figure 1.

2. Start the mass swinging by releasing it from a measured height of 1 m above its lowest point, as shown in Figure 1. Remember to keep the cord taut. Count the number of swings in 10 sec and multiply by 6 to obtain the number of swings in 1 min. Record your answer in the Data Table. Repeat twice more and take an average for the number of swings in 1 minute.

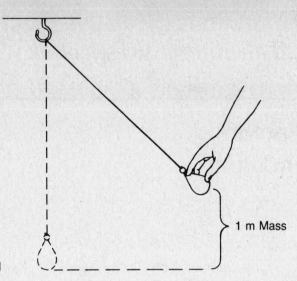

Figure 1

1 m Mass

3. Raise the pendulum to a height of 0.5 m above the lowest point. Release the mass, keeping the cord taut. Again, count the number of swings in 10 sec and multiply by 6 to obtain the number of swings in 1 min. Repeat twice more and take an average for the number of swings in 1 min. Record your answer in the Data Table.

4. Reduce the length of the cord by one half. Again, raise the mass 1 m over the lowest point, and keeping the cord taut, release the mass. Determine the average number of swings in 1 min, as you did in steps 2 and 3. Record your information in the Data Table.

5. Remove the 1-kg mass and replace it with a 0.5-kg mass. Raise the mass to a height of 1 m above its lowest point and, keeping the cord taut, release it. Determine the average number of swings in 1 min, as you did in steps 2, 3, and 4. Record your answer in the Data Table.

Observations

DATA TABLE

	Swings per Minute			
	Trial 1	Trial 2	Trial 3	Average
1-kg, full-length cord, 1 m high				
1-kg, full-length cord, 0.5 m high				
1-kg, half-length cord, 1 m high				
0.5-kg, full-length cord, 1 m high				
0.5-kg, full-length cord, 0.5 m high				
0.5-kg, half-length cord, 1 m high				

Analysis and Conclusions

1. By changing the height from which the mass is released in step 3, you change the length of the swing. How does the length of the swing affect the number of swings in 1 min?

   _____

2. How does the mass of the pendulum affect the number of swings in 1 min?

   _____

3. How does the length of the cord affect the number of swings in 1 min?

   _____

   _____

Critical Thinking and Application

1. Examine a pendulum on a grandfather's clock or a cuckoo clock. How could you adjust the pendulum to speed up a slow clock?

   _____

2. Based on what you know about free fall, why does the mass of a pendulum not affect the

   number of swings per minute? _____

   _____

   _____

3. If the length of the swing does not affect the number of swings per minute, what must happen to the speed of the pendulum as the length of the swing is increased?

   _____

4. How would the motion of a pendulum be different if the pendulum were on the moon

   rather than on the Earth? Why? _____

   _____

   _____

Going Further

   The direction in which a freely swinging pendulum moves is not affected by the rotation of the Earth. Construct a pendulum that will swing a long while by using a heavy weight and a long cord. What does the apparent movement (after 15 min or so) of the line of swing of the pendulum tell you about the Earth?

——— *Laboratory Investigation* ———

Chapter 16   Energy: Forms and Changes

42

Investigating Energy and Falling Motion

Background Information

When an object such as a ball falls, it accelerates and acquires kinetic energy, or energy of motion. If it does not reach terminal velocity, it acquires its maximum velocity and therefore its maximum kinetic energy just as it hits the ground. At that point, its motion is stopped and it is compressed. The kinetic energy is momentarily converted to potential energy, or stored energy. This potential energy is then converted back to kinetic energy as the ball bounces back. No ball will return to the exact height from which it was dropped because some of the kinetic energy is converted to other forms of energy, such as heat, when the ball strikes the ground. According to an important principle known as the law of conservation of energy, however, the total amount of energy does not change.

In this investigation you will describe the motion of a bouncing ball and examine how the ball demonstrates the law of conservation of energy. By plotting graphs, you will also examine how well different substances retain their original energy.

Problem

How can the motion of a bouncing ball be described and accounted for in terms of energy?

Materials *(per group)*

meterstick
tennis ball
Ping-Pong ball
sponge ball
air-filled rubber ball

Procedure

1. Have one member of your group hold the meterstick upright with the zero mark on the floor, as shown in Figure 1.

2. Have a second member of your group drop the tennis ball from the top of the meterstick (100-cm mark) in such a way that it does not touch the meterstick on the way down.

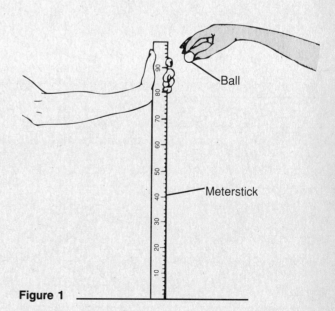

Figure 1

3. Have a third member of your group note the height of the first bounce. The bounce height should be called out to the fourth member of the group, who should record it in the Data Table. Let the ball continue to bounce and continue observing it for as long as you can. (It may take several trials because the ball may tend to bounce away from the meterstick.)

4. Repeat steps 1, 2, and 3 with the Ping-Pong ball, the sponge ball, and the air-filled rubber ball.

5. On Graphs 1 through 4, plot the height of each bounce for each ball. Draw a curved line that best fits through the vicinity of the points. You will plot four graphs.

Observations

DATA TABLE

Type of Ball	First Bounce	Second Bounce	Third Bounce	Fourth Bounce	Fifth Bounce	Sixth Bounce
Tennis						
Ping-Pong						
Sponge						
Air-filled rubber ball						

GRAPH 1 Tennis Ball

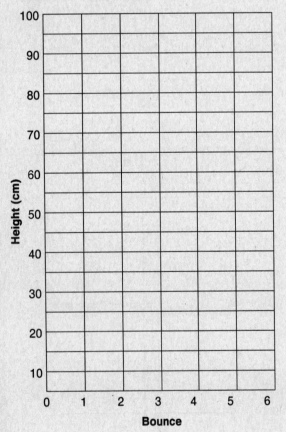

GRAPH 2 Ping-Pong Ball

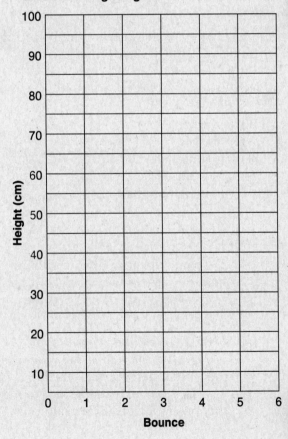

GRAPH 3   Sponge Ball

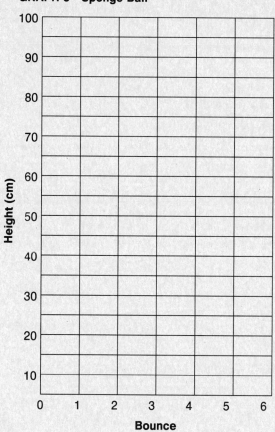

GRAPH 4   Rubber Ball

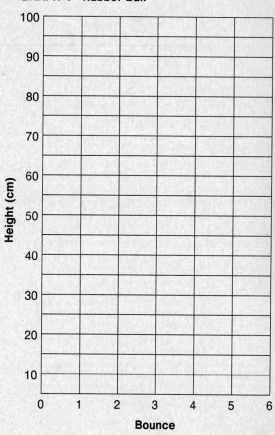

Analysis and Conclusions

1. Which ball retained the greatest percentage of its kinetic energy on each bounce?

_____

2. Explain the shape of each line on the graphs. Why were they similar?

_____

_____

3. What type of ball seems to bounce the least? Why?

_____

_____

_____

_____

_____

Critical Thinking and Application

1. Why can't a ball bounce higher than the height from which it is dropped?

_____

_____

2. Suppose you had carried out this investigation using a carpeted floor. How would your results have been affected? _____

_____

_____

_____

3. Explain your answer to question 2. _____

_____

_____

_____

4. What do you think would happen to the kinetic energy if a Ping-Pong ball collided with a sponge ball? _____

_____

_____

_____

_____

Going Further

1. Sometimes it is necessary to develop materials that will absorb kinetic energy, such as car bumpers and padded dashboards. Try to develop a container that will keep an egg from breaking if dropped from a great height. Remember, try to surround the egg with materials that will absorb the energy of the impact and not permit that energy to be transferred to the egg.

2. Conduct an experiment with two balls of similar materials suspended by cords. Pull the balls apart and let them collide with each other. How many bounces do they undergo before stopping?

_____ *Laboratory Investigation* _____

43

Investigating Heat Transfer

Background

The movement of heat is called heat transfer. There are three types of heat transfer: conduction, convection, and radiation. In conduction, heat is transferred through a substance or from one substance to another by the direct contact of one molecule with another. In convection, molecules of liquids or gases move in currents, transferring heat as they move. In radiation, heat energy is transferred through space.

Heat energy sets molecules in motion. And temperature is a measurement of that motion. In this investigation you will transfer heat energy from a fuel to water, causing the water to boil. You will then use the boiling water to transfer heat to cold water.

Problem

How is heat transferred?

Materials *(per group)*

4 100-mL beakers
100-mL graduated cylinder
Bunsen burner
heat-resistant gloves
tripod

wire gauze
Celsius thermometer
glass-marking pencil
safety goggles

Procedure

1. Label the four beakers 1, 2, 3, and 4. Into Beaker 1 pour 100 mL of tap water. Measure the temperature of the water and record it in the Data Table.

2. Place the beaker on a tripod covered with gauze. Put on your safety goggles. Position the Bunsen burner beneath the beaker and light it. **CAUTION:** *Be careful whenever lighting and using an open flame.* Heat the beaker until the water is boiling.

3. While the water in Beaker 1 is coming to a boil, pour 25 mL of tap water into both Beaker 2 and Beaker 3. Record the temperature of each beaker in the Data Table.

4. When the water in Beaker 1 is boiling, record its temperature. Shut off the Bunsen burner. Wearing heat-resistant gloves, carefully pour the boiling water from Beaker 1 into Beaker 2. Immediately record the resulting temperature of the mixed water in Beaker 2 in the Data Table.

5. Pour 50 mL of tap water into Beaker 4 and repeat step 2. When the water in Beaker 4 is boiling, record its temperature and shut off the heat source. Wearing heat-resistant gloves, immediately—but carefully—pour the boiling water into Beaker 3. Record the temperature of the resulting mixture in the Data Table.

Observations

DATA TABLE

Temperature of tap water in Beaker 1	_____°C
Temperature of boiling water in Beaker 1	_____°C
Temperature of tap water in Beaker 2	_____°C
Temperature of tap water in Beaker 3	_____°C
Temperature of water in Beaker 2 after water in Beaker 1 has been added	_____°C
Temperature of boiling water in Beaker 4	_____°C
Temperature of water in Beaker 3 after water in Beaker 4 has been added	_____°C

1. What was the temperature of the water immediately after mixing the boiling water in Beaker 2? In Beaker 3?

_____

2. What was the temperature change of the water in Beaker 2? In Beaker 3?

_____

3. What was the temperature change of the boiling water in Beaker 1 when it was mixed

with the tap water? _____ In Beaker 4? _____

Conclusions

1. Based on the temperature increases in Beakers 2 and 3, did Beaker 1 or Beaker 4 deliver

more heat? _____

2. The water in Beakers 1 and 4 was at the same temperature while boiling but did not contain the same amount of energy. Since the amount of water was not the same in Beakers 1 and 4 but the temperature was the same, what do you think temperature is

actually measuring? _____

_____

_____

_____

_____

_____

Critical Thinking and Application

1. When boiling water and tap water are mixed, how does the temperature of the mixture compare with the original temperatures of the water?

_____

2. Could the temperature of the mixture of boiling water and tap water ever reach the temperature of the boiling water? Explain.

_____

_____

3. Suppose 100 mL of boiling water is mixed with 100 mL of tap water. How would the temperature of this mixture compare with the temperature of a mixture of 100 mL of boiling water and 25 mL of tap water? Explain your answer.

_____

_____

4. Design an experiment in which you could investigate the temperatures of mixtures resulting from various proportions of boiling water and tap water.

_____

_____

Going Further

Boiling water does not always have the same temperature. The boiling temperature depends in part on the air pressure above the water. Find out why pressure is so important for determining the boiling point.

Laboratory Investigation

44

Heat of Combustion of a Candle

Background Information

Combustion is the process during which oxygen in the air reacts with a substance to produce heat and light. In this investigation you will determine the amount of heat produced when a candle burns. A device that measures heat is called a calorimeter. Your calorimeter will be a can of water. You will measure the temperature change and the amount of water that is heated in the can. The product of the mass of water heated and its temperature change is equal to the amount of heat in calories released by the burning candle.

Problem

How many calories of heat are released per gram by a burning candle?

Materials *(per group)*

296-mL tin can, open at one end
1.4-L tin can, open at both ends
tin can lid
candle
stirring rod
ring stand and ring
100-mL graduated cylinder
Celsius thermometer
ice cube
matches
balance
metric ruler
safety goggles

Procedure

1. Insert the glass stirring rod through the two holes in the small tin can. Hang the tin can by the stirring rod on a support ring as shown in Figure 1.

2. Attach the candle to the tin can lid with a few drops of melted wax. Place the candle under the hanging can. Measuring the distance with a ruler, adjust the can so it is 5 cm above the wick of the candle.

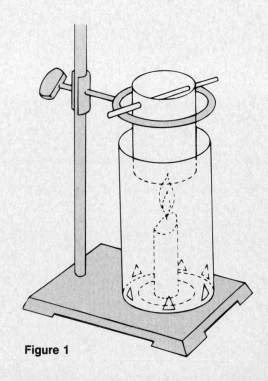

Figure 1

3. Remove the tin can and stirring rod.

4. Record the mass of the candle and lid to the nearest 0.1 g. Enter this value in the Data Table.

5. Replace the candle on the ring stand and place the large can over the candle, with the air vents at the bottom. See Figure 1.

6. Fill the small can half full with tap water. Cool the water with ice until the temperature drops to 10 to 15°C below room temperature. Remove any excess ice. Record the temperature to the nearest 0.1°C in the Data Table.

7. Light the candle. Immediately replace the can of water on the iron ring. **CAUTION:** *Be extremely careful when lighting and working with an open flame.*

8. Move the thermometer through the water very gently and note the temperature.

9. When the water temperature is about the same number of degrees above room temperature as it was below when the ice was added, blow out the candle.

10. Keep moving the thermometer through the water and record in the Data Table the highest temperature the water reached.

11. Find the mass of the candle and lid again. Record the mass in the Data Table.

12. Use the graduated cylinder to measure the volume of the water in the can. If the amount of water is greater than 100 mL, measure the first 100 mL and then measure the remaining water. Add the measurements together and record the mass in the Data Table.

Observations

DATA TABLE

Mass of candle + base before burning	_____ g
Lowest temperature	_____ °C
Highest temperature	_____ °C
Mass of candle + base after burning	_____ g
Volume of water	_____ mL

1. Calculate the change in temperature of water.

2. Calculate the amount of heat absorbed by the can of water. Heat in calories is the product of the mass of water and the change in temperature of the water. Since the density of water is nearly 1 g/mL, the mass of water is numerically equal to the volume of water. Therefore, the equation for heat is

   Heat = Volume of water × Temperature change

3. Calculate the mass of candle wax burned (Mass before burning − Mass after burning).

Conclusions

1. Calculate the heat released per gram of candle wax (heat absorbed by water divided by the mass of candle wax burned).

2. Was all of the heat released by the candle absorbed by the water? Explain your answer.

_____

_____

_____

Critical Thinking and Application

1. A certain candle has a mass of 15 grams. How much heat will be released when the candle burns to one third its original height?

2. How many grams of candle wax would be needed to heat 500 mL of water at 25°C to a temperature of 35°C?

3. A certain liquid X requires 0.5 calories per gram to have its temperature raised 1°C. Would 1 gram of candle wax produce enough heat to raise 1 kilogram of X 10°C?

Explain your answer. _____

_____

_____

4. Based on this investigation, suggest a method for determining the calorie content of a

certain food. _____

_____

_____

_____

Going Further

Repeat the procedure using a different-sized candle. Again calculate the heat required to burn 1 g of candle wax. Compare your answer with the answer obtained in the original procedure.

_____ *Laboratory Investigation* _____

Specific Heat

Background Information

When heat is transferred from a warmer object to a cooler one, the law of conservation of energy predicts that the amount of heat gained by the cooler object will equal the amount of heat lost by the warmer object. But the temperature increase of one object will not necessarily equal the temperature decrease of the other object. This is because objects differ in their *specific heat.* Specific heat is a measurement of the number of calories of heat needed to raise the temperature of an object by a certain amount. More specifically, the specific heat of an object is the number of calories needed to raise the temperature of 1 gram of the object 1 degree Celsius. The higher the specific heat, the more heat it takes to raise an object's temperature. The lower the specific heat, the greater the temperature change with the addition of heat.

In this investigation, a hot metal mass will be placed in cool water in a calorimeter. Heat will be transferred from the hot metal to the water, and the specific heat of the metal will be calculated.

Problem

How can specific heat be determined?

Materials *(per group)*

Celsius thermometer
triple-beam balance
calorimeter
hot plate
250-mL beaker
3 pieces of string, each 15 cm
  long
safety goggles
3 metal disks with hole:
  brass, lead, aluminum

Procedure

1. Put on safety goggles. Half fill the beaker with water and heat it to boiling on the hot plate. Proceed with the next step while waiting for the water to boil.

2. Find the mass of the calorimeter cup. Half fill the cup with tap water and determine the mass of the cup plus water. Calculate the mass of the cool water by subtracting the mass of the cup from the mass of the cup plus water.

3. Record the temperature of the cool water in the calorimeter in the Data Table.

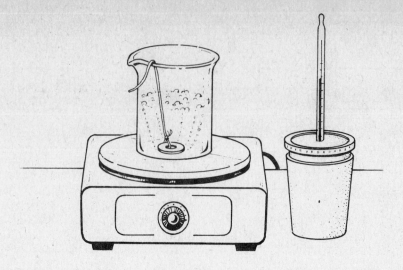

Figure 1

4. Measure the mass of one of the disks. Tie a piece of string around the disk and lower it into the boiling water so that the string hangs over the side of the beaker. Do not let the string touch the hot plate. Leave the metal disk in the boiling water for about 5 minutes to allow it to heat up to the same temperature as the water.

5. Measure and record the temperature of the boiling water. This will also be the temperature of the metal disk in the water.

6. Using the end of the string outside the beaker, remove the metal disk from the boiling water and *quickly* place it in the calorimeter cup. Cover the cup *immediately*. Note the thermometer reading. When the temperature stops rising, record this temperature as the final temperature of the water.

7. Calculate the change in temperature of the metal and the change in temperature of the cool water. Record these numbers in the Data Table.

8. Repeat steps 2 through 7 for the remaining metal disks.

Observations

DATA TABLE

	Brass	Lead	Aluminum
Mass of calorimeter			
Mass of calorimeter and water			
Mass of water			
Mass of metal			
Starting temperature of cool water			
Starting temperature of metal			
Final temperature of water			
Final temperature of metal			
Temperature change of water			
Temperature change of metal			

Conclusions

1. Calculate the heat gained by the cool water for each metal disk. Use the formula

$$\text{Heat gained by water} = \text{Mass of water} \times \text{Specific heat of water} \times \text{Change in temperature of water}$$

The specific heat of water is 1 cal/g·°C

a. Cool water with brass _____

b. Cool water with lead _____

c. Cool water with aluminum _____

2. Because the heat gained by the water in each case equals the heat lost by the metal, calculate the specific heat of each metal using the formula

$$\text{Heat lost by metal} = \text{Mass of metal} \times \text{Specific heat of metal} \times \text{Change in temperature of metal}$$

a. Brass _____

b. Lead _____

c. Aluminum _____

Critical Thinking and Application

1. The actual specific heats of the metals used in this investigation are brass, 0.09 cal/g·°C; lead, 0.03 cal/g·°C; aluminum, 0.22 cal/g·°C. How closely do the specific heats you calculated agree with these figures?

_____

_____

2. What three variables might have made your calculated results inaccurate?

_____

_____

_____

3. Water has one of the highest specific heats of any common substance, 1.0 cal/g·°C. Explain how this fact is related to the fact that shore areas tend to be cooler than inland areas in the summer and warmer than inland areas in the winter.

_____

_____

_____

4. The specific heat of ethanol is 0.59 cal/g·°C. If you spilled boiling alcohol on yourself, would there be any difference in the severity of that burn compared with the burn caused

by boiling water? _____ Explain your answer.

_____

_____

_____

Going Further

How would the results of this investigation be different if salt water or alcohol were used in place of tap water? State your hypothesis and design an investigation to determine if your hypothesis is correct. With your teacher's permission, perform the investigation and record your observations and conclusions.

Laboratory Investigation

46

Comparing Color and Radiation Absorption

Background Information

All hot objects, such as the sun, lighted lamps, and campfires, can transmit heat through space. This transmission can take place with or without the presence of molecules. Radiant heat energy is transmitted by the same mechanism as the transmission of radio waves and visible light. All such radiation is called electromagnetic radiation. The surface of the material being heated affects the degree to which radiant heat energy is absorbed by the material. Color is an important factor in heat absorption.

In this investigation you will use a thermometer to measure the amount of heat absorbed by different-colored surfaces and explain why one color does or does not absorb more heat than another. You will also graph and compare the change in temperature per unit time for the different surfaces. You will then be able to predict how shades of color on a surface affect the amount of heat absorbed.

Problem

What effect does color have on the ability of an object to absorb radiant heat energy?

Materials *(per group)*

100-W light source
2 coffee cans
heavy construction paper,
    1 white and 1 black sheet
corrugated cardboard, 12 cm ×
    12 cm
Celsius thermometer
classroom wall clock (with sweep
    second hand)
2 14-cm strips masking tape
2 different-colored pencils
scissors
ring stand and ring

Procedure

1. Cut the construction paper into rounds just larger than the opening of the coffee cans. Cover one of the coffee cans with the white paper circle and the other can with the black paper circle. Tape the edges with masking tape. See Figure 1.

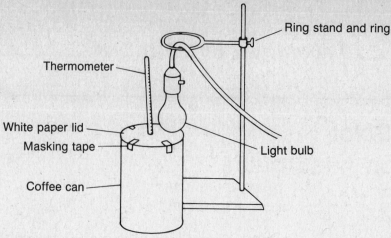

Figure 1

2. With a sharp pencil, carefully punch a hole in the centers of the construction-paper lids.

3. Carefully insert the thermometer bulb into the hole in the white lid.

4. Place this coffee can so that its lid is 5 cm beneath a 100-W lightbulb that is suspended by its wire from a ring stand and ring.

5. Switch on the lightbulb, which is a source of radiant energy. Record the temperature every 2 minutes for a period of 14 minutes in the Data Table. Switch off the light bulb after you have made the last observation.

6. Graph the data you have recorded for the white surface in colored pencil on the graph.

7. Carefully remove the thermometer from the white-lidded can and let the thermometer return to room temperature before starting with the black-lidded can.

8. Repeat steps 3 through 7 with the black-lidded can. Graph the data on the graph using a different-colored pencil.

Observations

DATA TABLE

White-Lidded Can		Black-Lidded Can	
Time (min)	Temp (°C)	Time (min)	Temp (°C)
0		0	
2		2	
4		4	
6		6	
8		8	
10		10	
12		12	
14		14	

GRAPH

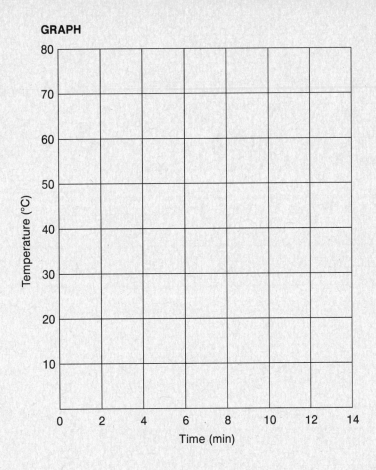

Conclusions

1. What effect does color have on the amount of radiant energy absorbed?

_____

2. What effect does color have on the rate at which radiant energy is absorbed?

_____

Critical Thinking and Application

1. In warm, sunny weather, what color clothing should people wear to stay cool? Why?

_____

_____

2. Design an experiment that could determine whether texture—in particular, shininess or dullness of surface—has any effect on the absorption of radiant energy. What effect

would you expect? _____

_____

_____

3. Many people have installed solar water-heating devices on the roofs of their houses. What color should these devices be in order to maximize their effect?

_____

4. What happens to the light rays that are not absorbed by light-colored objects?

_____

5. Based on your answer to question 4, explain why a skier standing on a ski slope on a sunny day feels warmer than when standing on a black-topped pavement.

_____

_____

_____

_____

Going Further

1. List applications of the fact that color affects absorption of radiant energy. One example is the color of ice-cream vending trucks. See how many such examples you can observe in one day.

2. Conduct an experiment with two identical coffee cans and thermometers. Leave one empty (actually, full of air) and fill the other with water. Which heats faster? Which cools faster?

_____ *Laboratory Investigation* _____

47 _____

Constructing a Solar Furnace

Background Information

As the cost of fossil fuels rises, many alternative sources of energy are being explored. One of these alternatives is solar energy. The sun is, directly or indirectly, the source of all energy on the Earth. The sun's energy can be directly used if harnessed properly. Many people have installed solar heating panels on the roofs of their houses. These devices are used to heat water for the people living in the building. Much research is being conducted in this area.

In order to maximize the energy from the sun, it is necessary to focus the sun's rays. Most often this is accomplished by using a curved mirrored surface, which reflects the rays back to a central point. Sometimes a magnifying lens accomplishes the same task by focusing the sun's rays to a point. A solar furnace is one example of this principle of focusing the sun's rays.

In this investigation you will construct a solar furnace with the capacity to boil water. A solar furnace is capable of developing high temperatures and should be treated with the same caution as a lighted Bunsen burner or an electric hot plate.

Problem

How does a solar furnace work?

Materials *(per group)*

automobile headlight reflector,
  with two holes punched in the
  rim
2 pieces of wood, about 3 cm
  wide, 1 cm thick, and 3 cm
  longer than the radius of the
  reflector (to be used as
  supports)
piece of wood, about 30 cm ×
  15 cm (for the base)
straight pins
cork large enough to fit
  snugly into the reflector hole
Pyrex test tube
wood screws

Procedure

1. Insert a wood screw into each hole with a washer and attach the reflector to the wood supports as shown in Figure 1.

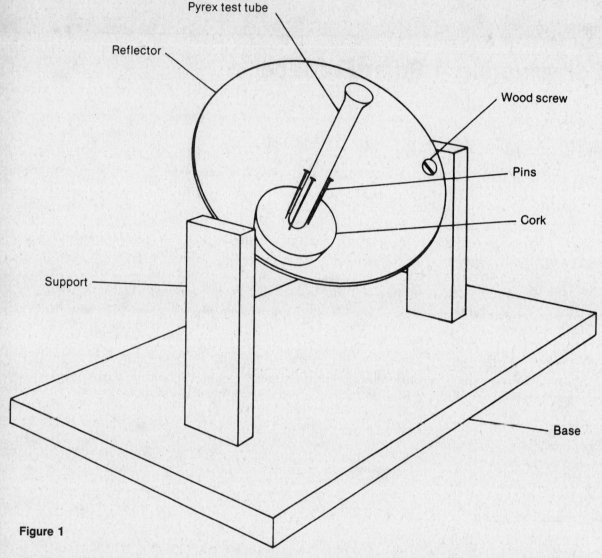

Figure 1

2. Attach the pieces of wood to the base with wood screws. At this point, check to be sure that the reflector can rotate easily on the wood screws. Tighten the screws just enough so that they can hold the reflector at any desired position.

3. Insert the cork into the hole intended for the bulb of the headlight. Make sure the cork fits tightly.

4. Insert the four pins into the cork in such a way that a test tube is held upright in the center of the reflector.

5. Aim the reflector toward the sun. All of the sun's rays should focus on the glass test tube.

6. When the reflector is in the proper position, stand behind the reflector and fill the test tube about one third full of water. Observe what happens.

Observations

1. In Drawing 1, trace the path of the sun's rays as they are reflected off the mirrored surface.

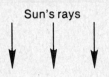

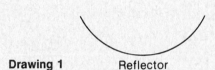

Drawing 1   Reflector

2. What happens to the water in the test tube? How long does this take?

_____

_____

Conclusions

1. Why does a reflector help the test tube get hot?

_____

_____

2. Do you think the water would become hot without the reflector? Explain.

_____

_____

_____

Critical Thinking and Application

1. Explain how the solar furnace could be improved to create even higher temperatures.

_____

_____

_____

2. Explain how your solar furnace could be used to change the sun's radiant energy into mechanical energy. _____

_____

_____

3. Why should you protect yourself from the sun on ski slopes and beaches?

_____

_____

_____

Going Further

    With adult supervision, devise a solar furnace using a magnifying lens. Attempt to position the lens in such a way that a large amount of sunlight is focused in a small area. **CAUTION:** *High temperatures can develop.*

_____ *Laboratory Investigation* _____

48 __

Conductors and Insulators

Background Information

When electrons move from place to place, an electric current is created. Not all materials allow electrons to flow through them. Materials that allow electrons to flow freely are called conductors. Materials that do not allow electrons to flow freely are called insulators. In this investigation you will test some common materials and determine which are electrical conductors and which are insulators.

Problem

Which materials are conductors and which are insulators?

Materials *(per group)*

1.5-V dry cell
1.5-V lamp with sockets
3 connecting wires, 30 cm long
test materials: penny (copper);
    dime (silver); paper; wax;
    glass; aluminum foil; plastic;
    paper clip; wood; rubber; cloth;
    pencil lead (carbon)

Procedure

1. Set up a dry cell, lamp, and connecting wires as shown in Figure 1. Have your teacher check your setup before proceeding.

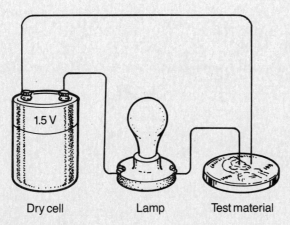

Dry cell   Lamp   Test material

Figure 1

2. Keep the ends of the two test wires about 2 cm apart. Bring the ends of the wires into contact with each of the materials to be tested. Record your observations in the Data Table.

3. After you have tested all of the materials, disconnect the wires from the dry cell.

Observations

DATA TABLE

Material	Relative Brightness		
	Bright	Dim	No Light
Copper			
Silver			
Paper			
Wax			
Glass			
Aluminum foil			
Plastic			
Paper clip			
Wood			
Rubber			
Cloth			
Carbon			

Analysis and Conclusions

1. Which of the materials you tested are good conductors of electricity? _____

_____

2. Which of the materials you tested are insulators? _____

_____

Critical Thinking and Application

1. Are metals electrical conductors or insulators? _____

2. Are nonmetals electrical conductors or insulators? _____

3. Why is most electrical wiring, such as the connecting wires you used in this investigation, made of copper? _____

_____

Going Further

Strip about 8 cm of wood from one side of a pencil to expose the lead core inside the pencil. Hold the two ends of your test wires as far apart as possible and touch them to the lead core. Slowly move the wires closer together and observe what happens to the lamp. Use what you have learned in this investigation to explain your observations.

Laboratory Investigation

49

Building Electric Circuits

Background Information

An electric circuit allows the flow of electrons from a power source to make a complete round trip back to the power source. Most electric circuits contain several elements such as lights, transformers, and switches. In a series electric circuit, only one path is available for the electrons to flow through. In a parallel electric circuit, two or more paths are available for the electron flow. In this investigation you will construct series and parallel circuits and measure their current and voltage.

Problem

How are the current and voltage of an electric circuit determined?

Materials *(per group)*

3 1.5-V lamps with sockets
1.5-V dry cell
21 connecting wires
0 to 1-A ammeter
0 to 3-V voltmeter
knife switch

Procedure
Part A   A Parallel Circuit

▪◧ **1.** Use the dry cell, connecting wires, and knife switch to connect the three lamps in parallel. See Figure 1. **Note:** *Be sure to connect the lamps to the dry cell and knife switch exactly as shown.* Make sure the knife switch is open. Post I must be connected to the positive terminal of the dry cell. Have your teacher check the circuit.

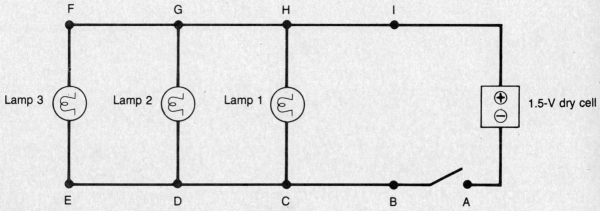

Figure 1

2. Close the knife switch and record your observation of the lamps.

_____

3. Unscrew the middle bulb. Record your observation.

_____

4. Retighten the middle bulb. Open the knife switch. Measure the total voltage of the circuit by placing the voltmeter as indicated in Figure 2. The positive terminal of the voltmeter must be connected to the positive post (I), and the negative terminal of the voltmeter must be connected to the negative post (B). Momentarily close the switch to see if the needle deflects to the right. If the needle deflects to the left, reverse the leads of the voltmeter. Record the total voltage (V_T) in the Data Table. Open the knife switch.

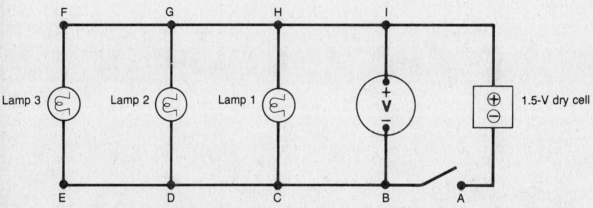

Figure 2

5. Measure the voltage across lamp 1 by connecting the positive lead of the voltmeter to post H and the negative lead to post C. Close the knife switch and record the voltage (V_1) in the Data Table. Open the switch.

6. Measure the voltage across lamp 2 by connecting the positive lead of the voltmeter to post G and the negative lead to post D. Close the switch and record the voltage (V_2) in the Data Table. Open the switch.

7. Measure the voltage across lamp 3 by connecting the positive lead of the voltmeter to post F and the negative lead to post E. Close the switch and record the voltage (V_3) in the Data Table. Open the switch and remove the voltmeter.

8. Measure the total current by removing the connecting wire between posts H and I and attaching the positive lead of the ammeter to post I and the negative lead of the ammeter to post H. See Figure 3. Momentarily close the switch. If the needle deflects to the left, open the switch and reverse the leads of the ammeter. Close the switch and record the total current (I_T) in the Data Table. Open the switch.

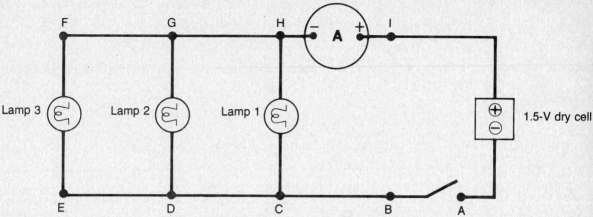

Figure 3

■■= **9.** Disconnect the ammeter and replace the connecting wire between posts H and I.
Disconnect the wire at post H that leads to lamp 1. Do not disconnect the wire at the
lamp. Connect the negative lead of the ammeter to the wire that is connected to the
lamp. Connect the positive lead of the ammeter to post H. See Figure 4. Close the
switch and record the current (I_1) through lamp 1 in the Data Table. Open the switch,
disconnect the ammeter, and reconnect the lamp wire to post H.

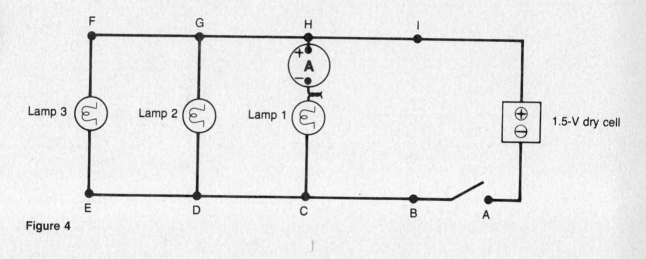

Figure 4

■■= **10.** Disconnect the lamp wire from lamp 2 at post G. Do not disconnect it at the lamp.
Connect the negative terminal of the ammeter to the lamp wire and the positive lead to
post G. Close the switch and record the current (I_2) through lamp 2 in the Data Table.
Open the switch, disconnect the ammeter, and reconnect the wire back to post G.

■■= **11.** Disconnect the lamp wire from lamp 3 at post F. Do not disconnect it at the lamp.
Connect the negative terminal of the ammeter to the lamp wire and the positive lead to
post F. Close the switch and record the current (I_3) in the Data Table. Open the switch,
disconnect the ammeter, and reconnect the lamp wire to post F.

Part B   A Series Circuit

▪▮= **1.** Connect the three lamps in series by removing the connecting wires between posts G and H, between E and D, and between C and B. Insert a connecting wire between posts E and B. Your circuit should now look like Figure 5. Have your teacher check your circuit. Close the switch and record your observation.

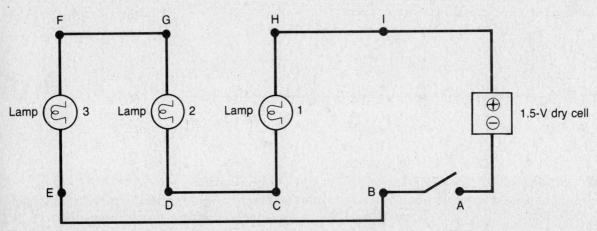

Figure 5

▪▮= **2.** Unscrew bulb 2 and record your observation. Tighten bulb 2 and open the switch.

▪▮= **3.** Connect the positive lead of the voltmeter to post I and the negative lead to post B. Close the switch. If the voltmeter deflects to the left, reverse the leads. Record the total voltage (V_T) in the Data Table. Open the switch.

▪▮= **4.** Connect the positive lead of the voltmeter to post H and the negative lead to post C. Close the switch and record the voltage (V_1) across lamp 1 in the Data Table. Open the switch.

▪▮= **5.** Connect the positive lead of the voltmeter to post D and the negative lead to post G. Close the switch and record the voltage (V_2). Open the switch.

▪▮= **6.** Connect the positive lead of the voltmeter to post F and the negative lead to post E. Close the switch and record the voltage (V_3) in the Data Table. Open the switch and remove the voltmeter.

▪▮= **7.** Measure the total current by removing the connecting wire between posts H and I and connecting the positive lead of the ammeter to post I and the negative lead of the ammeter to post H. Close the switch. If the needle deflects to the left, reverse the leads. Record the total current (I_T) in the Data Table. Open the switch, remove the ammeter, and replace the connecting wire between posts H and I.

▪▮= **8.** Disconnect the wire from lamp 1 at post C. Do not disconnect this wire at the lamp. Connect the positive lead of the ammeter to the lamp wire and the negative lead to post C. Close the switch and record the current (I_1) through lamp 1 in the Data Table. Open the switch, disconnect the ammeter, and reconnect the lamp wire to post C.

•◫᷄ **9.** Disconnect the wire from lamp 2 at post G. Do not disconnect it from the lamp. Connect the positive lead of the ammeter of the lamp wire and the negative lead to post G. Close the switch and record the current (I_2) in the Data Table. Open the switch, disconnect the ammeter, and reconnect the lamp wire to post G.

•◫᷄ **10.** Disconnect the wire from lamp 3 at post E. Connect the positive lead of the ammeter to the lamp wire and the negative lead to post E. Close the switch and record the current (I_3) in the Data Table. Open the switch, disconnect the ammeter, and reconnect the lamp wire to post E.

Observations

DATA TABLE

Circuit	Voltage (volts)				Current (amps)			
	V_T	V_1	V_2	V_3	I_T	I_1	I_2	I_3
Parallel								
Series								

Analysis and Conclusions

1. Add the currents I_1, I_2, and I_3 in the parallel circuit. Is the total current (I_T) approximately equal to the sum of the three individual currents in a parallel circuit?

   _____

   _____

2. Add the voltages V_1, V_2, and V_3 in the parallel circuit. Is the total voltage equal to the sum of the individual voltages in a parallel circuit?

   _____

   _____

3. In a parallel circuit, is the total voltage equal to the individual voltages?

   _____

   _____

4. Add the currents I_1, I_2, and I_3 in the series circuit. Does the total current equal the sum of the individual currents in a series circuit?

   _____

   _____

5. Is the total current approximately equal to the individual currents in a series circuit?

_____

_____

6. Add the voltages V_1, V_2, and V_3 in the series circuit. Is the total voltage approximately equal to the sum of the individual voltages in a series circuit?

_____

_____

7. In which circuit would a burned-out bulb cause all the other bulbs to go out?

_____

Critical Thinking and Application

1. Explain why all the bulbs in a series circuit go out when one bulb is disconnected.

_____

_____

2. Voltage is the force or "push" that gets electrons moving. Based on your data, explain why the bulbs in a series circuit burn dimmer than the bulbs in a parallel circuit.

_____

_____

_____

3. What would happen to the current in a parallel circuit if all the bulbs were not the same

size? _____

_____

Going Further

Why are the lamps in a house lighting circuit not connected in series? Explain your answer.

_____ *Laboratory Investigation* _____

Properties of Magnets and Magnetic Fields

Background Information

Although magnets come in a variety of shapes and sizes, the simplest type of magnet is a straight bar made of iron. Like all magnets, a bar magnet has two ends, or poles: a north magnetic pole and a south magnetic pole. Magnetic forces are strongest at these poles. Surrounding the magnet is a magnetic field in which magnetic forces are also felt.

In this investigation you will use simple bar magnets and some iron filings to explore magnetism and magnetic fields.

Problem

What is a special property of magnets? How can you observe a magnetic field?

Materials *(per group)*

2 bar magnets
thread
2 pieces of wood, 10 cm long
index card
iron filings

Procedure
Part A   Properties of Magnets

1. Tie a piece of thread around the center of one bar magnet.

2. Hold the magnet by the thread so that the magnet can turn freely, as shown in Figure 1.

3. Bring the south pole of the other bar magnet near the south pole of the hanging magnet. Observe what happens.

4. Now bring the north pole of the magnet near the south pole of the hanging magnet. Observe what happens.

Figure 1

Part B   Observing a Magnetic Field

1. Place a bar magnet between the two pieces of wood.

2. Cover the magnet with an index card. See Figure 2.

3. Sprinkle iron filings on top of the card. Gently tap the card several times to distribute the iron filings evenly. Observe what happens.

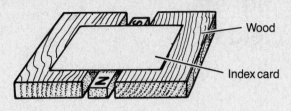

Figure 2

Observations

1. What happened when you brought the south pole of a bar magnet near the south pole of the hanging magnet?

   _____

2. What happened when you brought the north pole of the bar magnet near the south pole of the hanging magnet?

   _____

   _____

3. What happened when you sprinkled iron filings on the card over the bar magnet? _____

   _____

Analysis and Conclusions

1. What is a special property of magnets by which they can be identified? _____

   _____

2. What is the shape of the magnetic field around a bar magnet, as shown by the pattern of

   iron filings? _____

   _____

3. Where is the magnetic field strongest? _____

   How can you tell? _____

   _____

Critical Thinking and Application

1. What rule describes the behavior of magnetic poles? _____

_____

2. How could you make the hanging bar magnet rotate without touching the magnet? _____

_____

_____

_____

_____

3. Why does the magnetic field around a bar magnet form an arc between the north and

south poles of the magnet? _____

_____

_____

Going Further

Repeat Parts A and B of this investigation using magnets of different shapes and sizes. To make a permanent record of the magnetic field in Part B, use light-sensitive paper in place of the index card.

_____ *Laboratory Investigation* _____

Studying Electromagnetic Induction

Background Information

In 1831, Michael Faraday discovered that when a coil of wire is moved in a magnetic field, an electric current is generated, or induced, in the wire. This process is called electromagnetic induction. Electromagnetic induction involves cutting across magnetic lines of force.

In this investigation you will use a bar magnet and a magnetic compass with a coil of wire wrapped around it to detect an electric current in the wire. When an electric current flows through the coil of wire, the compass needle will move.

Problem

How can you create an electric current by moving a coil of wire in a magnetic field?

Materials *(per group)*

compass
bar magnet
connecting wire, 4 m

Procedure

1. Using a piece of wire 1 m long, wrap 20 loops of wire around the compass, as shown in Figure 1.

2. Place the compass on a table or other flat surface. Align the compass needle with the wire.

3. With the remaining 3-m length of wire, wind 10 loops of wire around your finger. The coil should be large enough for the bar magnet to fit through.

4. Connect the two coils of wire by twisting the ends of the wires together. The second coil should be at least 1 m away from the compass.

5. Slowly push the north pole of the bar magnet into the coil of wire. Observe what happens to the compass needle.

6. Remove the magnet and add 10 more loops of wire to the coil. Repeat step 5.

7. Slowly push the south pole of the magnet into the coil of wire. Observe what happens to the compass needle.

8. Observe what happens to the compass needle as you slowly pull the magnet out of the coil of wire.

9. Repeat step 5, but this time push the magnet into the coil quickly.

Compass

Bar magnet

Figure 1

Observations

1. What happened when you slowly pushed the north pole of the bar magnet into the coil

of wire? _____

_____

2. What happened to the compass needle after you added 10 more loops of wire to the coil

and pushed the north pole of the magnet into the coil? _____

_____

3. What happened when you pushed the south pole of the magnet into the coil of wire? ____

_____

4. What happened when you pushed the magnet into the coil quickly? _____

_____

Analysis and Conclusions

1. Explain what you observed happening when you moved a magnet in a coil of wire. _____

_____

_____

_____

_____

2. What is this process called? _____

Critical Thinking and Application

1. How does the number of loops of wire affect the current in the wire? _____

_____

2. How did changing the pole of the magnet affect the direction of the current in the wire?

How can you tell? _____

_____

_____

3. Would a current be induced in the wire if you did not move the magnet? Why or why

not? _____

_____

4. Would a current be induced if you moved the coil of wire instead of the magnet? Why or

why not? _____

_____

_____

Going Further

What do you think would happen if you made a coil of wire by turning 10 loops of wire in one direction and 10 loops in the opposite direction? Try it and find out.

_____ Laboratory Investigation _____

52

Constructing a Telephone

Background Information

The operation of the telephone involves energy conversions. In the transmitter of the telephone, sound waves are converted into electric waves that travel over wires. In the receiver of the telephone, electric waves are converted back into sound waves.

The first telephone conversation took place on March 10, 1876 between the inventor of the telephone, Alexander Graham Bell, and his assistant, Thomas Watson.

In this investigation you will build a simple device that illustrates the operation of a telephone transmitter.

Problem

How do carbon grains in the transmitter of a telephone affect the flow of electricity?

Materials (per group)

plastic cup
1.5-V lamp with sockets
carbon grains
2 copper strips

2 alligator clips
1.5-V dry cell
3 connecting wires,
  30 cm long

Procedure

1. Place the two copper strips in either side of the plastic cup.

2. Half fill the cup with carbon grains.

3. Using an alligator clip, connect one end of a wire to one of the copper strips. Connect the other end of the wire to one side of the lamp socket.

4. Connect another wire to the other side of the lamp socket. Connect the other end of this wire to one of the dry cell poles.

5. Using an alligator clip, connect a third wire to the other copper strip. Connect the other end of the wire to the other dry cell pole. See Figure 1.

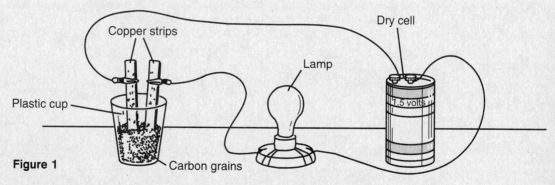

Figure 1

6. Squeeze the copper strips together, then let them go.

Observations

1. What happens when you squeeze the copper strips together?

_____

2. What happens when you stop squeezing the copper strips together?

_____

Analysis and Conclusions

1. How does pressure on the carbon grains affect the flow of electricity?

_____

_____

2. How does this investigation illustrate the operation of a telephone transmitter?

_____

_____

_____

_____

_____

Critical Thinking and Application

1. How is the pressure on the carbon grains in a telephone transmitter regulated?

_____

_____

2. How is the operation of a telegraph similar to that of a telephone?

_____

How is it different? _____

_____

Going Further

Find out what new technology is being used in telephone communication.

Laboratory Investigation

Constructing a Simple Computer Circuit

Background Information

Computers use combinations of off-on (flip-flop) circuits to perform their various functions. A circuit that is on represents the number 1. A circuit that is off represents 0. The binary number system (base 2) has only two numbers—1 and 0. The computer uses the binary system to represent all numbers, letters, and commands. In this investigation you will construct an electric circuit that will convert decimal (base 10) numbers into binary (base 2) numbers.

Problem

How does an off-on computer circuit work?

Materials *(per group)*

3 1.5-V lamps with sockets
1.5-V dry cell
3 knife switches, single pole-single
    throw
knife switch, double pole-single
    throw
connecting wires
pegboard
machine screws
12 clips or screws for connecting
    wires

Procedure

◀▮▶ **1.** Connect the lamps, switches, and dry cell on the pegboard as shown in Figure 1. Note that switch 3 must have two separate poles so it can be connected to both lamps 1 and 2.

2. Have your teacher check your circuit before you proceed.

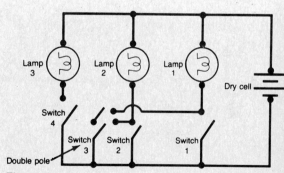

Figure 1

⊣⊢ 3. Switches 1, 2, 3, and 4 correspond to the decimal numbers 1, 2, 3, and 4. Close switch 1 and record which lamps are lit and which remain off. Record a 1 if lit, 0 if off. For example, if only the middle lamp is lit, record 010.

4. Open switch 1.

⊣⊢ 5. Repeat steps 3 and 4 for switch 2, then switch 3, and finally switch 4. Record each result in the Data Table.

Observations

DATA TABLE

Decimal	Binary
1	
2	
3	
4	

Analysis and Conclusions

1. Your circuit converted decimal (base 10) numbers to binary (base 2) numbers. Do your results in the Data Table agree with the following decimal-binary conversion chart?

Decimal	Binary
1	001
2	010
3	011
4	100
5	101
6	110
7	111

_____

_____

2. Only the first four decimal numbers were converted to binary numbers. Explain how you could convert the following decimal numbers to binary numbers using your circuit.

a. 5   b. 6   c. 7

If time permits, try these numbers on your circuit.

_____

_____

Critical Thinking and Application

1. What is the largest decimal number your circuit can convert? Why?

   _____

   _____

2. What would you have to do to your circuit to go beyond this number?

   _____

   _____

3. What is the product of binary numbers 101 $\times$ 010? Write your answer in binary

   numbers. _____

4. What is the value of binary number 111101?

   _____

Going Further

   Each lamp corresponds to a bit on a computer. Each number or letter on a keyboard is represented as a byte. Find out how many bits make a byte. How many lamps would be required to represent a byte in your circuit?

Name _____ Class _____ Date _____

Laboratory Investigation

54 ___

Creating a Computer Program

Background Information

The use of computers is becoming more and more evident in our daily life. They are extremely helpful in performing very complex tasks at great speed. In order for any computer to be used efficiently, it must be properly programmed. A program is a series of instructions placed in the computer's memory. These instructions order the computer to perform tasks and to make simple yes or no decisions.

Computer program designers must be able to think clearly and analyze the task to be done. They must be able to break down a complex task into simple ones. These simple tasks must be sequenced in the correct order. New information must be processed at just the right time.

In order to help analyze any task, program designers create flowcharts to describe and sequence the parts of a task. Various shaped boxes are used in a flowchart as symbols for different functions. See Figure 1.

(Start or Stop)   *Start or Stop box* describes the beginning or end of a program.

/ Input or Output /   *Input or Output box* describes a step to input information or to write out some information.

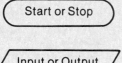

Computation or Assignment box describes a computation to be carried out or assigns a new value to some item in the program.

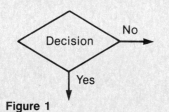

Decision box describes a yes or no decision. Program makes decision on the basis of the answer.

Figure 1

In this investigation you will learn how to change a computer task into a flowchart using the flowchart symbols given.

Problem

How are computers programmed?

Materials *(per student)*

    paper
    pencil

Procedure

1. Study the task indicated by the following question: "Is the combined age of the males in a certain family greater than the combined age of the females?"

2. Study the flowchart example in Figure 2, which shows you how to solve this task.

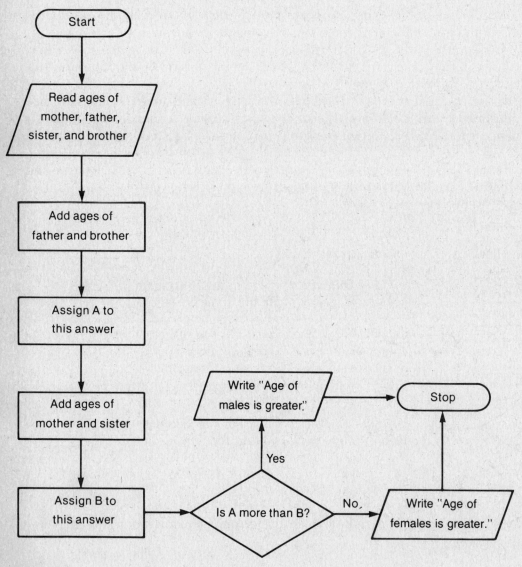

Figure 2

3. Write flowcharts in the space provided for Drawings 1 and 2 for the following questions. Use the symbols you have learned and the example shown in Figure 2.

   a. Is the average of three test grades a passing mark (65 is passing)?

   b. What is the cost of X kilograms of potatoes at Y cents per kilogram, and can a man with Z cents afford to buy them?

Observations

1. For question 3a, what information must be inputed? _____

   _____

2. What decision must the computer make in question 3a?

   _____

   _____

   _____

   _____

3. How many different pieces of information must be inputed in question 3b? What are

   they? _____

   _____

   _____

   _____

   _____

Analysis and Conclusions

Drawing 1

Drawing 2

Critical Thinking and Application

1. Study the flowchart you made in Drawing 2. What would happen to your program if the first assignment box were left out? _____

_____

_____

_____

2. In Drawing 2, what would happen to your program if you forgot to multiply X by Y?

_____

_____

_____

_____

3. A student running a program based on Drawing 1 finds that nearly every combination of test grades comes out passing, unless the sum of the grades is less than 65. What is probably wrong with the program? _____

_____

_____

_____

4. A student wants to see if a man with $1.50 can buy 2 kg of potatoes at 75 cents per kilogram. The student runs the program and finds that the man cannot afford the potatoes. What might the student have done wrong?

_____

_____

_____

_____

Going Further

1. Learn how the binary number system can be used by a computer to make rapid electrical calculations.

2. Devise a flowchart for a program to play tic-tac-toe so that the computer never loses.

————————— *Laboratory Investigation* —————————

Chapter 23 Characteristics of Waves

55

Waves and Wave Motions

Background Information

Although all waves are not the same, they have many characteristics in common. Sound waves, light waves, water waves, and other types of waves are similar in both properties and behavior.

In this investigation you will study the behavior of water waves in a ripple tank. Your observations of the water waves will also apply to other types of waves.

Problem

What are the properties of moving waves?

Materials *(per group)*

ripple tank
light source
wood blocks
glass square (1.2 cm thick)
30-cm ruler
rubber hose or bendable metal
    strip to fit tank
large sheets of white paper
medicine dropper

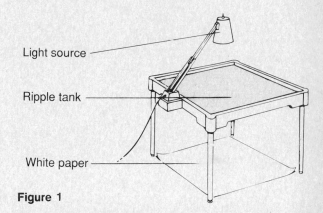

Light source

Ripple tank

White paper

Figure 1

Procedure

1. Set up the ripple tank as indicated in Figure 1.

2. Add water to a depth of 1.5 cm.
   As you perform steps 3 through 10, draw a diagram of what you see in each step in the space provided in Observations. Label your diagram according to the directions below:
      The crest of a wave should be drawn as a line.
      The direction in which the waves move should be shown by an arrow.
      The point of origin of the wave should be marked with an o.
      Any barrier that stops the wave should be marked with a b.

3. Place the ruler on its side in the tank and slowly move it back and forth a distance of about 1 cm. Draw the wave pattern and write a brief description of it under your diagram.

4. Repeat step 3 but move the ruler back and forth more rapidly. Draw the wave pattern and write a brief description.

5. Place the wood blocks in the tank so that they form a barrier at an angle to the side of the tank. Slowly move the ruler back and forth as in step 3. Note the angle at which the waves bounce off, or are reflected from, the barrier. Draw the wave pattern and write a brief description.

6. Place the section of hose or metal strip in the ripple tank so that it forms a curved barrier. Move the ruler back and forth in the tank as in step 3. Draw the wave pattern both going toward the curved surface and reflected from it. Write a brief description.

7. Remove all objects from the ripple tank. When the water is still, use the medicine dropper to slowly let water droplets fall into the center of the ripple tank. Draw the wave pattern and write a brief description of it.

8. Use the wood blocks to form a barrier at an angle to one of the sides of the tank. Repeat step 7. Draw and describe the wave pattern.

9. Place the curved hose or metal strip in the tank as in step 6. When the water is still, let water droplets fall into the center of the tank as in step 7. Draw and describe the wave pattern.

10. Place the glass square in the pan near one side of the tank so that the sides of the square are parallel to the sides of the tank. Slowly move the ruler back and forth. Draw and describe the wave pattern.

Observations

Step 3

Step 4

Step 5

Step 6

Step 7

Step 8

Step 9

Step 10

Analysis and Conclusions

1. What type of waves were generated by the back-and-forth motion of the ruler?

   _____

2. What type of waves were generated by the drops falling into the ripple tank?

   _____

3. How did the waves generated in steps 3 and 4 differ from each other?

   _____

   _____

4. What is the relationship between the frequency and wavelength of a wave?

   _____

   _____

   _____

5. In step 5, how did the angle at which the waves hit the barrier compare with the angle at

   which they were reflected? _____

   _____

6. How did the waves reflected from the straight surface differ from the waves reflected

   from the curved surface? _____

   _____

   _____

7. How is the behavior of the waves generated by the water drop different from that of the

   waves generated by the ruler? _____

   _____

   _____

   _____

Critical Thinking and Application

1. Do the waves generated by the movement of the ruler represent longitudinal waves or

   transverse waves? _____ Explain. _____

   _____

   _____

2. Do the waves generated by the falling droplets of water represent longitudinal waves or

   transverse waves? _____ Explain. _____

   _____

   _____

3. Were there any differences in the behavior of the waves formed by the moving ruler and

   those formed by the droplets of water? _____ Explain. _____

   _____

   _____

4. Review the diagrams you drew as part of your observations. In which diagram(s) did you
   observe the following wave interactions?

   a. Reflection _____

   b. Refraction _____

   c. Diffraction _____

   d. Interference _____

Going Further

Repeat the above investigation generating waves from two sources (rulers or droppers) at
the same time. Draw and describe the wave patterns formed. How do these wave patterns
differ from the wave patterns formed in this investigation?

Laboratory Investigation

56

Determining the Speed of Sound

Background Information

Sound travels at different speeds through different materials. This is because some materials transmit sound better than others. Liquids transmit sound much faster than gases do. For example, sound travels about four and one half times faster through water than through air. If you have ever been swimming in a pool, you may have noticed that sound is transmitted faster under water. Many solids are even better sound transmitters. Temperature also affects how rapidly sound is transmitted. Sound will travel faster in warm air than in cold air. However, the speed of sound does not depend upon the frequency of the sound. If it did, you would not be able to listen to music because the high-pitched sounds would arrive at your ear at a different time than the low-pitched sounds.

The speed of light is much greater than the speed of sound. You may have had the experience of seeing a lightning flash and then, seconds later, hearing the thunder. The lightning and thunder occur at the same time, but the sound of the thunder takes much longer to reach your ears. You will use this principle to calculate the speed of sound. You will perform an experiment similar to one performed by French scientists in 1738. They set up a cannon on a hill and timed the interval between the flash and the sound. Since they knew the distance and the time, they could calculate the speed of sound.

In this investigation you will determine the speed of sound in air.

Problem

How can the speed of sound be determined?

Materials (*per group*)

drum
stopwatch capable of timing to a
    tenth of a second
measuring rope marked off in
    meters

Procedure

1. This experiment must be conducted outdoors. Select an area such as an open field or a long, lightly traveled road.

2. With the measuring rope (or a bicycle equipped with a metric odometer), measure a distance of 100 m in a straight line.

3. One pair of students should stand at the beginning of this measured distance and the other at the end, as shown in Figure 1.

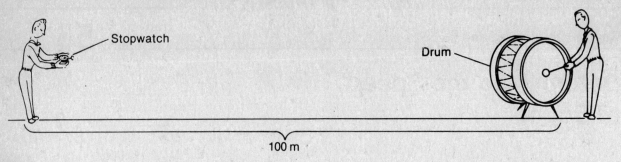

100 m

Figure 1

4. The first pair of students should create a loud, short noise by striking the drum.

5. The other pair of students should start the stopwatch precisely when they see the drum being struck. They should stop the watch precisely when they hear the noise.

6. Make two trials and record the times to a tenth of a second in the Data Table.

7. Change places with the other group and repeat the experiment. (This will eliminate any effect of wind in one direction.) Record your results in the Data Table.

Observations

DATA TABLE

Trial	Time (sec)
1	
2	
3	
4	

Analysis and Conclusions

1. Average the four times and calculate the speed of sound by dividing the distance by the average time. _____

2. What factors might have caused variations in the results of your four trials?

_____

_____

_____

Critical Thinking and Application

1. Explain how you could determine how far from you lightning struck if you knew the speed of sound and had a stopwatch. _____

_____

_____

2. When fireworks burst in the sky, will you hear the explosion or see the color first? Explain. _____

_____

3. In early movies, the sounds spoken by the characters on the screen did not match the movement of their lips, but instead lagged behind. Based on this investigation, suggest a possible explanation for this. _____

_____

_____

_____

4. Sound travels faster in liquids than in gases, and faster in solids than in liquids. Explain why a worker who puts one ear against a long metal pipe would hear two sounds if another worker struck the pipe only once at some distance away.

_____

_____

Going Further

Suspend a bell or alarm clock inside a large jar from which air can be evacuated by a pump. Observe what happens to the sound of the bell or alarm as the air is sucked out. Observe the speed of sound through other materials such as water or iron.

_____ *Laboratory Investigation* _____

Getting the Most
From the Sun

Background Information

Most of the energy received and used on Earth comes from the sun. Although the most obvious form of the sun's energy is the light you see, this is only part of the sun's electromagnetic energy. Much of the energy is in the form of ultraviolet waves and infrared waves. This is why sunlight makes you feel warm.

In this investigation you will measure the heating effects of the sun and see how different materials change these effects.

Problem

How can the amount of energy obtained from sunlight be increased and decreased?

Materials *(per group)*

3 identical jars
black paper
aluminum foil
tape
3 Celsius thermometers
sand

Procedure

1. Fill each of the three jars with sand.

2. Wrap one jar completely with black paper, including the top, and tape the paper in place.

3. Cover the second jar with aluminum foil, including the top, and tape the foil in place.

4. Record the temperature on each of the three thermometers. Be sure all three indicate the same temperature.

5. Insert one thermometer into the sand in each jar. With the two covered jars, puncture a hole in the top covering and insert the thermometer through the hole.

6. Place all three jars in direct sunlight.

7. Record the temperature of each of the thermometers every 15 minutes for about 2 hours.

Observations

Time (min)	Temperature of Jar 1 Uncovered (°C)	Temperature of Jar 2 Covered in Black (°C)	Temperature of Jar 3 Covered in Foil (°C)
0			
15			
30			
45			
60 (1 hr)			
75			
90			
105			
120 (2 hr)			

Analysis and Conclusions

1. What is the purpose of the uncovered jar?

_____

_____

_____

2. How do the temperatures of the thermometers compare over time?

_____

_____

_____

3. How is the energy of sunlight carried to the sand in the jars? What type of electromagnetic radiation is mostly responsible for heating the sand?

_____

_____

_____

_____

4. What can you say about the effect of a black surface and a shiny surface on absorption of energy from the sun?

_____

_____

_____

Critical Thinking and Application

1. Would the investigation have had the same conclusions if you had used a material other than sand? Explain.

_____

_____

_____

2. Certain materials are designed to take advantage of the properties you saw in this investigation. For example, the glass windows of many buildings are coated with a thin layer of silver to keep the inside of the building cool. What are other black and silver materials and what are their uses?

_____

_____

_____

_____

3. On a sunny day, would you expect the interior of a black car or a silver car to be warmer? Explain.

_____

_____

_____

_____

4. Using what you have learned from this investigation, explain why astronauts wear silver clothing in space.

_____

_____

_____

Going Further

Remove the jars from the sunlight and continue to record the temperatures of the three thermometers for 2 more hours. How do the temperatures compare? What can you say about the effect of a black surface and a shiny surface on heat loss?

Laboratory Investigation

58

Plane Mirror Images

Background Information

The image of an object formed by a plane, or flat, mirror seems to be exactly like the object. But is the image really an exact "copy" of the object? And how does a mirror produce an image?

In this investigation you will see how a plane mirror forms an image and how that image compares to the object.

Problem

How is an image produced by a plane mirror?

Materials _(per student)_

cardboard (approximately
   30 cm × 30 cm)
30-cm ruler
3 straight pins
protractor
unlined paper
small mirror and
   support

Procedure

⚗ **1.** Place the paper on the cardboard. Stand the mirror in the center of the paper and draw a line along the edge of the mirror. Stick a pin in the paper and cardboard about 4 cm in front of the mirror. Draw a small circle around the pin position and label it Object. See Figure 1.

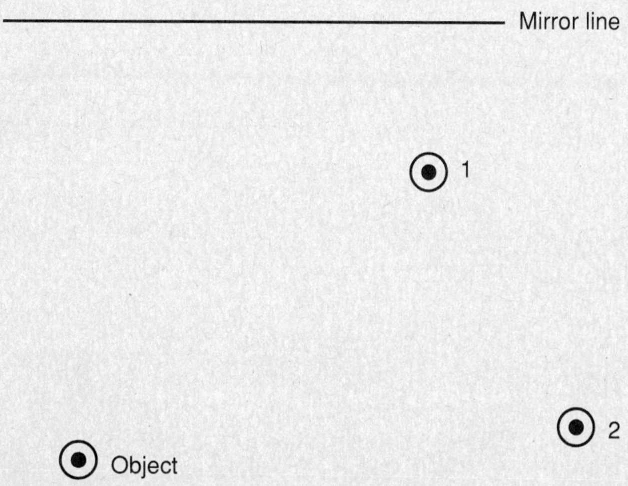

_____ Mirror line

⊙ 1

⊙ 2

Figure 1   ⊙ Object

2. Bend down so that your head is near the lower right corner of the paper. Look at the mirror with one eye closed and observe the reflection of the pin. Do not look at the real pin. Place a pin in the paper so that it hides the reflection of the object pin in the mirror. Draw a small circle around the pin position and label it 1.

3. From the same position on the righthand side of the paper, place a second pin in the paper so that it hides the real pin you placed in position 1 and the reflection of the object pin. Draw a small circle around the pin position and label it 2.

4. Remove the pins from positions 1 and 2. Use them to repeat steps 2 and 3 from the lower left corner of the paper. Draw circles around these pin positions and label them 3 and 4.

5. Remove the mirror and all the pins. Using the ruler, draw a solid line through pin positions 1 and 2 and extend it as far as the mirror line. This line is a reflected ray. Draw a line from the object position to the point where the reflected ray leaves the mirror. This line is the incident ray. Label each ray and use an arrow on the ray to show its direction.

6. Repeat step 5 for pin positions 3 and 4.

7. Draw two lines perpendicular to the mirror line at the two points where the incident rays and the reflected rays touch. These lines are the normals. Label and measure the angles of incidence and reflection for the rays coming from the left and right corners of the paper. See Figure 2.

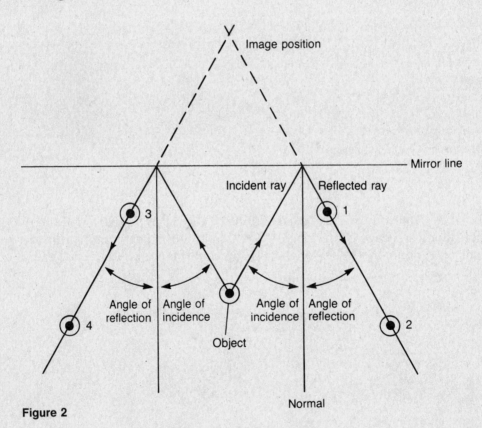

Figure 2

8. Using the ruler, draw two dashed lines extending the two reflected rays beyond the mirror line. Continue your dashed lines just beyond the point where they cross. This point is the position of the image of the pin in the mirror. Label this point Image.

Observations

1. Attach your drawing.

2. Left-side rays: Angle of incidence = _____ Angle of reflection = _____

3. Right-side rays: Angle of incidence = _____ Angle of reflection = _____

Analysis and Conclusions

1. At what distance is the object from the mirror line? _____

2. At what distance is the image from the mirror line? _____

3. How do the distances of the object and image from the mirror compare?

   _____

4. How do the angle of incidence and the angle of reflection compare in size

   a. for the rays from the left side of the paper? _____

   b. for the rays from the right side of the paper? _____

Critical Thinking and Application

1. Follow the path of one of the incident rays to the mirror and of its reflected ray. Repeat for the other incident ray. If the incident ray enters from the left, the reflected ray leaves

   toward the _____. If the incident ray enters from the right, the reflected ray

   leaves toward the _____.

2. Based on your answer to question 1, how does the image compare with the object?

   _____

3. If the angle of incidence were not equal to the angle of reflection, would that have an

   effect on the appearance of the image? _____ Explain. _____

   _____

   _____

4. When you look in a plane mirror, the image seems to be "inside" or "behind" the mirror. Yet an examination of the mirror reveals that the back is opaque. That is, no light rays can pass through it. What kind of image is not formed by real light rays?

_____

Why does the image seem to be "inside" or "behind" the mirror?

_____

_____

_____

_____

Going Further

Investigate the types of images formed by convex and concave mirrors. How do the images formed by these curved mirrors compare to the actual objects? Find some practical applications of these mirrors.

_____ *Laboratory Investigation* _____

59

Refraction of Light

Background Information

You have probably observed that a pencil in a half-filled glass of water appears to be broken at the point where the air and water meet. This happens because rays of light passing from one substance into another substance of different density change their direction of motion. The rays bend, or refract. An observer sees the light rays bend as they pass from one substance to another. In the case of the "broken" pencil, the rays of light coming from the pencil in the water bend as they pass from the water to the air. As a result, the pencil appears to be broken.

In this investigation you will observe the refraction, or bending, of light as it passes through a glass plate having parallel sides.

Problem

How do light rays behave as they pass through substances of different densities?

Materials *(per student)*

cardboard (approx. 30 cm × 30 cm)
glass plate (7 cm × 7 cm × 6 cm thick)
4 straight pins
protractor
ruler
unlined paper

Procedure

⚠ 1. Place the paper on the cardboard. Place the glass plate in the center of the paper so that the transparent edges are at the top and bottom. Draw a line around the glass plate.

2. Using your ruler, draw a line on your paper at an angle to the top of the glass plate. Do not draw this line perpendicular to the plate. See Figure 1.

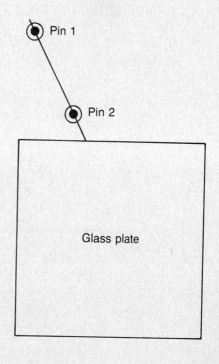

Figure 1

3. Place two pins on the line about 3 cm apart. Draw circles around the base of the pins and label the circles Pin 1 and Pin 2. Bend down and look through the bottom edge of the glass plate until you see Pins 1 and 2 positioned exactly behind each other. (They will look like only one pin.)

4. Place two more pins on the lower part of your paper so that they also seem to line up with Pins 1 and 2. (All four pins should appear to be one pin.) Draw circles around the base of these pins and label them Pin 3 and Pin 4.

5. Remove the pins and the glass plate. Using a ruler, draw a line through the positions of Pins 3 and 4 just to where they meet the line made by the glass plate.

6. The line through Pins 1 and 2 represents a ray of light entering the glass plate and is called the incident ray. Label this ray and draw arrows on it to show its direction of motion.

7. The line through Pins 3 and 4 represents a ray of light leaving the glass plate and going to your eye. It is called the emergent ray. Label this ray and draw arrows on it to show its direction of motion.

8. Using your ruler, connect the incident ray and the emergent ray through the glass plate. This line is called the refracted ray. Label this ray and draw arrows on it to show its direction of motion.

9. Using a protractor, construct perpendiculars to the side of the glass plate at the points where the incident and emergent rays touch it. These lines are called normals. Extend the normals into the glass plate area. You should have formed two angles on each side of the glass plate.

10. Two angles are formed with the normal as the incident ray touches the side of the plate and as the refracted ray touches the side of the plate. These two angles are called angles of incidence. Label these two angles I.

11. Two angles are formed with the normal as the refracted ray moves through the glass plate and again as the emergent ray leaves the plate. These two angles are called angles of refraction. Label these two angles R.

12. Measure the angles of incidence and the angles of refraction and record your measurements in Observations.

13. Using your ruler and a dashed line, extend the emergent ray backward through the glass plate and beyond it.

Observations

1. Attach your completed ray diagram.

2. Pins 1 and 2: Angle of Incidence _____ Angle of Refraction _____

3. Pins 3 and 4: Angle of Incidence _____ Angle of Refraction _____

Analysis and Conclusions

1. As the incident ray enters the glass, how does it bend with respect to the normal?

_____

2. As the emergent ray leaves the glass, how does it bend with respect to the normal?

_____

3. How do the two angles of incidence compare?

_____

4. How do the two angles of refraction compare?

_____

5. What do the emergent ray and the incident ray have in common?

_____

Critical Thinking and Application

1. Why does the light ray bend as it passes from air to glass or from glass to air?

_____

_____

_____

_____

2. In this investigation, the refracted ray can also be the incident ray. Why? *Hint:* Turn the

drawing upside down. _____

_____

_____

_____

3. Suppose you try to retrieve a coin that has fallen into an aquarium. Looking down into the water, you see the coin and reach for it, but find it is not where it appears to be.

Why? _____

_____

_____

_____

Going Further

Repeat this investigation using a glass triangle instead of a square glass plate. Measure the angles of incidence and refraction as you did in this investigation. How do the angles of incidence and refraction compare? How do your results compare with those for the square glass? Form a hypothesis to account for any differences you might observe.

_____ *Laboratory Investigation* _____

60

Observing Refraction of Light

Background Information

When light passes at an angle from air to a denser substance such as glass, the light rays bend. The bending of light is called refraction. Lenses refract, or bend, light. Convex lenses, which are thicker in the middle than at the edges, cause light to converge at a focal point. Concave lenses, which are thinner in the middle, cause light to diverge, or spread out.

The images formed by refracted light are either real or virtual images. Real images can be focused on a screen. Virtual images cannot. In this investigation you will compare the images formed by convex and concave lenses.

Problem

How do convex and concave lenses refract light?

Materials (*per group*)

convex lens with focal point of
    10–15 cm
concave lens
image screen
light source
meterstick with support stands
lens holder
light source holder
screen holder

Procedure

1. Set up the optical bench as shown in Figure 1. Use the convex lens. How can you tell

which is the convex lens? _____

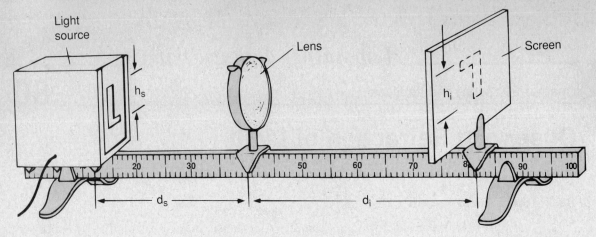

Light source

Lens

Screen

h_s

h_i

d_s

d_i

Figure 1

2. Determine the focal length of your lens by removing the light source and pointing the lens and screen toward an unshaded window. Slide the screen along the meterstick until a clear image of an outside tree, car, house, or other object is visible. Measure in centimeters the focal length (distance between the screen and the lens). Record the focal length in the Data Table.

3. Place the screen at one end of the meterstick and the light source at the opposite end.

4. Slide the lens until it is 5 cm more than twice the focal length from the light source. Slide the image screen along the meterstick until a well-defined image appears. Record the following in the Data Table: (a) whether the image is erect or inverted; (b) distance (d_s) from the light source to the lens; (c) distance (d_i) from the lens to the image; (d) height (h_s) of the light source; (e) height (h_i) of the image.

5. Repeat step 4, but this time slide the lens until it is exactly twice the focal length from the light source. Be sure to record the results in the Data Table.

6. Repeat step 4 again, but this time slide the lens until it is less than two focal lengths but more than one focal length from the light source. Record your results in the Data Table.

7. Position the lens so that it is exactly one focal length from the light source. Can an

image be formed? _____

8. Position the lens less than one focal length from the light source. Can an image be

formed? _____

9. Remove the screen and look at the light source through the lens.

Observation _____

10. Replace the convex lens with the concave lens. Repeat step 9.

Observation _____

11. Slide the lens 10 cm farther from the light source.

Observation _____

260

Observations

DATA TABLE

Focal length of lens: ___				
d_s (cm)	d_i (cm)	h_s (cm)	h_i (cm)	Erect or Inverted

Analysis and Conclusions

1. As the distance (d_s) between the convex lens and the source decreased, did the distance (d_i) between the lens and the image decrease or increase?

_____

2. As d_s decreased, did the height (h_i) of the image decrease or increase?

_____

3. At what distance (d_s) must the lens be placed in order for the image height (h_i) to be equal to the source height (h_s)? Express your answer in terms of the number of focal lengths (1f, 2f, 2.5f). _____

4. Can a real image be produced when the lens is placed at or less than a focal length's distance from the source? _____

5. Does the concave lens produce a real or a virtual image?

_____

6. Does the size of the image in a concave lens increase or decrease as the lens is moved away from the source? _____

Critical Thinking and Application

1. Explain how the lenses in eyeglasses help nearsighted and farsighted people see better.

_____

_____

_____

2. Why might a photographer have to change lenses when taking a close-up shot?

_____

_____

_____

3. An optical instrument is producing upside-down images. What might be the problem?

_____

_____

_____

4. How might lenses be used to produce the images in a funhouse mirror?

_____

_____

_____

Going Further

Find out what kind of lens is used in a refracting telescope and how it operates to produce an image of a distant object.

Laboratory Investigation

61

Constructing a Pinhole Viewer and a Periscope

Background Information

Light travels in straight lines. This enables scientists to predict its behavior during reflection and refraction. Many instruments and devices make use of this property. In this investigation you will construct two such devices: a pinhole viewer and a periscope.

Part A   Pinhole Viewer

Problem

How does a pinhole viewer work?

Materials (*per group*)

small juice or coffee can (with plastic top, if possible) with a small (approximately 1 mm), clean, round hole punched into the center of the closed end

rubber band
piece of waxed paper or tracing paper slightly larger than the open end of the can

candle and matches
piece of cardboard (6 cm × 6 cm)

Procedure

1. Hold the can up to your eye and look through it. Make certain the hole punched in it is small, clean, and centered.

2. Place the piece of translucent waxed or tracing paper over the open end of the can and use the rubber band to fasten it in place.

3. Light the candle and place a few drops of wax on the small piece of cardboard. Then place the candle onto it so that it will remain upright.

4. Position the candle and cardboard on the top of the lab table.

5. Hold the pinhole viewer so that the pinhole points toward the lighted candle. Position the viewer so that an image of the candle is clearly seen on the translucent paper screen. (Lights in the classroom may have to be shut off and the shades drawn for this part of the lab investigation.) Draw the image of the lighted candle in Drawing 1.

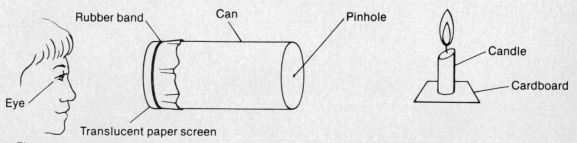

Figure 1

Observations

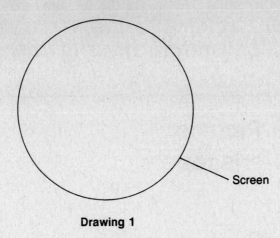

Screen

Drawing 1

Analysis and Conclusions

1. Is the image in Drawing 1 right side up or upside down?

_____

2. If the lighted candle is so much larger than the pinhole, how is it that the image is

   formed on the translucent screen? _____

_____

_____

Critical Thinking and Application

1. How could this pinhole viewer be changed into a pinhole camera? Be as specific as you

   can. Include drawings if you wish. _____

_____

_____

2. In Drawing 2, draw what you think is the path the rays of light take from the lighted
   candle to form the image on the translucent screen. Use a straight edge (ruler) when you
   draw the rays of light.

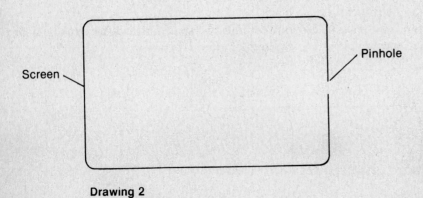

Screen

Pinhole

Candle flame

Drawing 2

Part B   Periscope

Problem

How does a periscope work?

Materials *(per group)*

scissors
oak tag (heavy grade)
2 small pocket mirrors
rubber cement

Procedure

1. Draw the solid lines on the oak tag as shown in Figure 2.

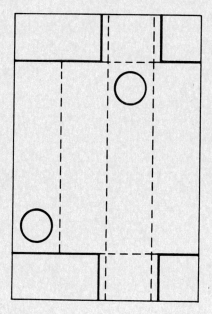

Figure 2

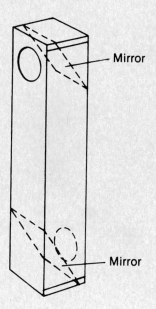

2. Using the scissors, carefully cut along the solid lines to create the frame and openings for your periscope.

3. Fold the oak tag along the dotted lines as shown in Figure 2.

4. Using rubber cement, glue the small mirrors in place before gluing the top and bottom closed.

5. Test your periscope by getting below the level of your desk or laboratory table and sighting the candle. You might also see if you can observe objects around corners or out in the corridor.

Observations

Draw the way light rays travel
in a periscope in Drawing 3.

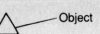

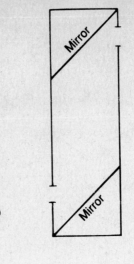

Drawing 3

Analysis and Conclusions

1. Does a periscope demonstrate that light travels in straight lines, even though it enables you to see around corners? Explain your answer.

_____

_____

2. What would happen to the image if only the mirror near the opening of the periscope

were used? _____

_____

Critical Thinking and Application

1. What must be true about the angles of the two mirrors used in a periscope? Why?

_____

_____

2. Suppose you are hiking along the side of a mountain and want to send a flashlight signal to someone who has just rounded a bend in the trail. How might you do it?

_____

_____

_____

Going Further

1. Develop a pinhole camera that has a shutter and a film holder on the back. Use a cartridge-type film. Take pictures of objects in bright sunlight.

2. Make a device that is a combination of a pinhole camera and a periscope that will enable you to take a picture of an object even though it is not directly in your sight.